THE
BOOK
ON
LEADERSHIP

JOHN
MACARTHUR

THOMAS NELSON
Since 1798

NASHVILLE   DALLAS   MEXICO CITY   RIO DE JANEIRO   BEIJING

Published in Nashville, Tennessee, by Thomas Nelson. Thomas Nelson is a registered trademark of Thomas Nelson, Inc.

Published in association with the literary agency of Wolgemuth & Associates, Inc.

Nelson Books titles may be purchased in bulk for educational, business, fund-raising, or sales promotional use. For information, please e-mail SpecialMarkets@ThomasNelson.com.

Unless otherwise noted, Scripture quotations are from THE NEW KING JAMES VERSION, © 1979, 1980, 1982 by Thomas Nelson, Inc., Publishers.

Scripture quotations noted NASB are from the NEW AMERICAN STANDARD BIBLE®, © The Lockman Foundation 1960, 1962, 1963, 1968, 1971, 1972, 1973, 1975, 1977, 1988, 1995. Used by permission.

Scripture quotations noted NIV are from the HOLY BIBLE: NEW INTERNATIONAL VERSION. © 1973, 1978, 1984 by International Bible Society. Used by permission of Zondervan Publishing House. All rights reserved.

Scripture quotations noted KJV are from the KING JAMES VERSION of the Bible.

The map on page 16 was created by Phil Johnson.

Cover design by David Uttley
UDG|DesignWorks, Inc.

Interior design and typeset by Katherine Lloyd, The DESK

Library of Congress Cataloging-in-Publication Data

MacArthur, John, 1939–
    The book on leadership / John MacArthur.
        p. cm.
    Includes bibliographical references.
    ISBN 978-0-7852-6251-0 (hardcover)
    ISBN 978-0-7852-8838-1 (trade paper)
    1. Christian leadership. 2. Christian leadership—Biblical teaching. 3. Bible. N.T.—Criticism, interpretation, etc. 4. Paul, the Apostle, Saint. I. Title.
    BV652.1.M23 2004
    253—dc22

                                                                            2004020084

Printed in the United States of America

09 10 11 12 13 QW 12 11 10 9 8 7

CONTENTS

INTRODUCTION

What makes a leader?

Rank? Status? Celebrity? Caste? Clout? Style?

Is leadership automatically bestowed by a box on the organizational chart? Where do position and power figure into the formula for leadership? And what is the ideal model for leaders? Is it the corporate CEO? The military commander? The head of state?

Jesus answered all those questions in a few words. His views on leadership are conspicuously out of step with the conventional wisdom of our age: "You know that the rulers of the Gentiles lord it over them, and those who are great exercise authority over them. Yet it shall not be so among you; but whoever desires to become great among you, let him be your servant. And whoever desires to be first among you, let him be your slave— just as the Son of Man did not come to be served, but to serve, and to give His life a ransom for many" (Matthew 20:25–28).

According to Christ, then, the truest kind of leadership demands service, sacrifice, and selflessness. A proud and self-promoting person is not a good leader by Christ's standard, regardless of how much clout he or she might wield. Leaders who look to Christ as *their* Leader and their supreme model of leadership will have servants' hearts. They will exemplify sacrifice.

I realize those are not characteristics most people associate with leadership, but they are essential qualities of a *biblical* approach to leadership, which is the only kind I'm interested in.

Notice, by the way, that Jesus was expressly teaching Christians to approach leadership in a different way and from a radically different point of view than the leaders of this world. It's folly for Christians to assume (as these days many do) that the best way for Christians to learn leadership is from worldly examples.

There's a crucial reason for this: Leadership for the Christian *always* has a spiritual dimension. The duty of leading people carries with it certain spiritual obligations. That is as true for the Christian president of a secular company as it is for the stay-at-home mom whose sphere of leadership might extend no further than her own children. All Christians in every kind of leadership are called to be *spiritual* leaders.

I'll be speaking about the spiritual dimension of leadership throughout this book, but please don't imagine that I'm writing only to pastors, career missionaries, or church leaders. Every leader who is also a Christian—including the manager of the widget factory, the football coach, and the public-school kindergarten teacher—needs to remember that the leadership role is a spiritual responsibility, and the people we lead are a stewardship from God, for which we will one day be called to give an account (cf. Matthew 25:14–30).

If you truly understand your accountability before God as a leader, you can begin to see why Christ portrayed the leader as a servant. He was *not* suggesting, as many have supposed, that lowliness alone is the essence of leadership. There are plenty of humble, meek, tenderhearted, servant-minded people who are not *leaders*. A true leader inspires followers. Someone who has no followers can hardly be called a leader.

So while it is certainly true that leadership demands a servant's heart; it is by no means the case that everyone with a servant's heart is thereby a leader. There's far more to leadership than that.

To put it simply, leadership is *influence*. The ideal leader is someone whose life and character motivate people to follow. The best kind of leadership derives its authority first from the force of a righteous example, and not merely from the power of prestige, personality, or position. By contrast, much of the world's "leadership" is nothing but manipulation of people by threats and rewards. That is not true leadership; it's exploitation. Real leadership seeks to motivate people from the inside, by an appeal to the heart, not by external pressure and coercion.

For all those reasons, leadership is not about style or technique as much as it is about character.

Want proof that effective leadership is not just about *style*? Notice that a number of divergent leadership styles are modeled in Scripture. Elijah was a loner and a prophet; Moses delegated duties to trusted people whom he kept close to him. Peter was brash; John was tenderhearted. Paul was a dynamic leader, even when being carried about in chains. He influenced people primarily through the force of his words. Evidently, his physical appearance was anything but powerful (2 Corinthians 10:1). All were men of action, and all used their diverse gifts in markedly different ways. Their leadership styles were varied and diverse. But all were true leaders.

Again, I think it's a serious mistake for Christians in leadership to pass over these biblical examples of leadership and turn instead to secular models of leadership in pursuit of style-obsessed formulae they think will make them better leaders. Yet entire organizations now exist to train church leaders with leadership techniques and management styles gleaned from worldly "experts." I recently read a Christian book that analyzes the entrepreneurial and administrative techniques used at Google.com, Amazon.com, Starbucks, Ben & Jerry's, Dell Computers, General Foods, and several other prestigious secular corporations. The authors of that book occasionally try to insert a biblical proof-text or two to buttress some of the principles they teach, but for the most part, they uncritically accept whatever seems to produce "success" as a good model for church leaders to imitate.

Then someone gave me an article from *Forbes*. The publisher of that magazine says a best-selling book on church leadership and ministry philosophy by an evangelical pastor is "the best book on entrepreneurship, business and investment that I've read in some time."[1] The *Forbes* publisher says, "Whatever you think about [this pastor] or his religious beliefs, he has

discerned a consumer need out there." Then he gives a brief summary of
the book, substituting the word *business* for *church,* to demonstrate that the
same management principles currently producing megachurches will work
in the corporate world. Ironically, he is quoting a pastor who has borrowed
his philosophy from successful secular entrepreneurs. The assumption is
being made on both sides that whatever "works" in the corporate realm is
automatically transferable to the church and vice versa. For example, the
Forbes editor quotes the pastor: "Faith and dedication won't overcome a
lack of skill and technology. Funny words from a preacher, but how true."[2]

But is that *really* true? Are faith and dedication lacking something vital
that must be supplied by skill and technology? Has modern management
theory suddenly unlocked principles of leadership that were hidden until
now? Does the financial success and corporate growth of McDonald's
automatically make their approach to McManagement a good model for
Christian leaders to follow? Does the clout of Wal-Mart translate into
proof that their corporate leadership style is *right*? Is authentic leadership
merely a matter of technique? Can this approach of mimicking whatever is
currently fashionable in secular management theory possibly be reconciled
with Jesus' statement that His kingdom operates by a markedly different
style of leadership from "the rulers of the Gentiles"?

Of course it can't. It is a serious mistake for Christians in positions of
leadership to be more concerned with what is currently popular in the corporate world than with what our Lord taught about leadership. I'm
convinced that the leadership principles He taught are essential to authentic success in both spiritual and secular realms. And just because a
leadership technique seems to "work" effectively in a corporate or political
environment doesn't mean it ought to be embraced uncritically by
Christians. In other words, you don't become a *spiritual* leader by studying
the techniques of corporate CEOs. You can't exemplify *biblical* leadership
and follow the trends of Madison Avenue at the same time. There's much
more to Christlike leadership than modus operandi. Again, true *spiritual*
leadership is all about character, not style.

That is my theme in this book. I'm convinced there are *better* models for Christian leaders to follow than Ben and Jerry. Surely our mentors in spiritual leadership ought to be spiritual people. Doesn't it seem obvious that the apostle Paul would have more to teach Christians about how to lead than we could ever learn from Donald Trump? For that very reason, this book is based largely on biographical material from the life of the apostle Paul from the New Testament.

From the time I was in junior high school, I have devoured various biographies of great Christian leaders—eminent preachers, distinguished pastors, prominent missionaries, and other heroes of the faith. Their lives fascinate and challenge me. I'm strongly motivated by men and women who have served Christ well. Their stories have been a powerful catalyst for me to move ahead in my own spiritual walk. Collectively, they have influenced me as much as any living, breathing influence I have ever been exposed to. Of course, I am the sum of many influences, not the least of which would include my father's godly example as a pastor and preacher of the Word, my mother's pattern of prayer and holy living, and many other personal spiritual mentors who have taught me. But I cannot discount the profound impact on my life that has come from biographies written about people I will never meet face-to-face this side of heaven.

Our culture today is crying for pragmatic solutions, easy formulas, three-step, four-step, or twelve-step programs to answer every human need. Certainly the hunger for practical answers is not entirely wrong. Although biblical exposition has always been my primary aim and methodology in my own preaching and writing ministry, I *do* try to be as practical as possible in my teaching. (The book you hold in your hands includes a long list of twenty-six practical principles for leaders. See the Appendix.)

But I have always found Christian biography to be inherently practical. A book that expounds the history or career of a noble Christian doesn't usually need to be enhanced with explicit how-to steps or imperatives and admonitions directed at the reader. The testimony of a godly life by itself is sufficient to motivate. That is why I treasure the life stories and memoirs of godly leaders.

Of all the biographies I have read and the lives that have left their mark on my character, no one mortal individual has left a deeper impression on me than the apostle Paul. I sometimes feel I know more about him than anyone else except Christ, because I have spent a major portion of my life studying the biblical account of his life, letters, and ministry, learning leadership at his feet.

I spent several years in the 1990s preaching through 2 Corinthians, which includes some of the most significant autobiographical material on Paul in all of Scripture. No epistle and no portion of the book of Acts exposes Paul's true heart with the same clarity or passion as that often-overlooked epistle. It is more than autobiographical; it is a very personal look into the depths of his soul. It is a picture-window perspective into the character of a Christian who is a leader and who walks closely with God. It reveals what a person can be who truly looks into the face of Jesus Christ. Here is a model for those who want to be *spiritual* leaders. Here is the pattern. Here is the flesh-and-blood example and my mentor.

Therefore I have based most of this book on autobiographical and biographical material drawn from Acts 27 and 2 Corinthians. These passages show Paul at his best as a leader. Some who merely scan these pages might be tempted at first to think, *This is all about Paul; it's not really about me.* But it's actually about what we *ought* to be. Paul himself said, "I urge you, imitate me" (1 Corinthians 4:16). "Imitate me, just as I also imitate Christ" (11:1). He was a true example of the Christlike leader.

We'll start with several chapters examining how Paul's leadership was manifest in the most unlikely of situations—in a shipwreck, where he was the lowest-ranking person onboard ship. And yet he rose to the occasion and demonstrated extraordinary powers of leadership.

The second part of the book will examine principles of leadership from several key passages in 2 Corinthians. My interest in leadership was heightened and my understanding of leadership principles was sharpened when I preached through that wonderful epistle. As we shall see, it is filled with keen insight on how to lead people.

The third part of the book rounds out our study of leadership with two key passages, one from 1 Corinthians 9:24–27 and one from Acts 6:1–7. These two closing chapters feature key insights about the leader's character and personal discipline.

What we learn from the apostle Paul is the same thing Jesus taught: that character—not style, not technique, not methodology, but *character*—is the true biblical test of great leadership. Entrepreneurship is wonderful, but the most skilled entrepreneur in the world without character is no true leader. Strategic planning is important, but if you don't have leaders whom people will follow, your strategic plan will fail. The clarity of a well-drafted purpose statement is crucial, but the true spiritual leader must go beyond merely clarifying people's focus. The real leader is *an example to follow*. And the best example to follow, as Paul knew, is the one who follows Christ.

Therefore Scripture, not the corporate world or the political arena, is the authoritative source we need to turn to in order to learn the truth about spiritual leadership. That approach, I hope, is what will stand out as the chief distinctive of this book.

Of course, for the Christian, biblical principles must also then be taken back and applied in the corporate realm, in family life, in politics, and in all of society. Biblical principles of leadership are not principles for the church only. In fact, Christians ought to be the trend-setters for all secular, corporate, and political leadership, rather than thoughtlessly borrowing from the world whatever seems to "work."

I have written this book with all kinds of leaders in mind. I've already written other books that deal specifically with church leadership and ministry philosophy. That's not my aim here. Instead, my goal in this book is to distill the biblical principles of leadership in a way that I hope will be beneficial for leaders in every realm—business leaders, civic leaders, church leaders, parents, teachers, personal disciplers, youth leaders, or whatever.

Is everyone supposed to be a leader? Obviously, not everyone is called to be a leader at the same level, or leadership by definition would not exist (cf. 1 Corinthians 12:18–29). But every Christian is called to be a leader of sorts, at some level, because all of us are given a mandate to teach and to influence others. Christ's Great Commission is a command to "make disciples of all the nations . . . teaching them to observe all things that [Christ has] commanded" (Matthew 28:19–20). The writer of Hebrews rebuked his readers for their spiritual immaturity, saying, "You ought to be teachers" (5:12). Clearly, then, all Christians are called to influence others and teach them the truth about Christ. Therefore, no matter what your status, position, giftedness, or occupation, you are called to be a leader at some level.

So this book is for you, whether or not you currently think of yourself as a "leader." My prayer is that you will aspire to the kind of leadership the apostle Paul exemplified: bold, uncompromising, faithful, *spiritual* leadership that inspires people with a hunger to be imitators of Christ.

PART 1

PAUL IN CHAINS: LEADERSHIP IN ACTION

Chapter One

EARNING TRUST

A crisis of leadership faces both the world and the church. As I write these words, the headlines in the secular press are all about leaders in the corporate world who have been guilty of appalling moral negligence. They have bankrupted major corporations because of their own personal greed. They have engaged in illegal insider trading. They have lied, cheated, stolen, and swindled. The scope and scale of corporate corruption in the world today are almost inconceivable.

In the political realm, the picture may be even more bleak. The moral scandals that rocked the Clinton White House changed the climate of American politics. The lesson of that episode (as far as some politicians are concerned) seemed to be that a person can lie and cheat and lack moral integrity—and yet not necessarily forfeit his career as a politician. Personal integrity, apparently, is no longer a requirement for political office. In the post-Clinton culture, a serious moral indiscretion seems to be no significant impediment to candidates for public office.

In the visible church, sadly, things are little better. The televangelist scandals of the 1980s seem to be all but forgotten. Nothing much really changed in the wake of the scandals. If anything, the state of so-called "Christian" television is far worse than it was before. Most Christian TV celebrities are still making greedy, nonstop appeals for money. Christian recording artists keep embarrassing the church with scandalous moral failures. And we still regularly hear of pastors who discredit their ministries and disqualify themselves by defaulting in the one thing that matters most in leadership: character.

Both church and world seem to have traded away the notion of leadership for celebrity. Today's heroes are people who are famous for being famous. They are not necessarily (and not even *usually*) men and women of character. Real leadership is in seriously short supply.

In a sense, however, the leadership vacuum presents a tremendous opportunity. The world is crying out for leaders—great heroic, noble, trustworthy leaders. We need leaders at every level of the social order—from political leaders in the international realm to spiritual leaders in the church and the family.

And most people recognize that need. I recently attended a special meeting of college presidents at the University of Southern California. At the same time, a conference on leadership was being held in an adjacent hall. We all mingled during the lunch hour. A table was set up in the lobby, displaying dozens of recent books on leadership. As I listened to the discussions and perused the book table, I realized that the severity of the current leadership crisis is common knowledge. How to *solve* the crisis, however, seems to be a puzzle to most, even to some of the most powerful men in the academic world.

Could it be that people don't *see* how the leadership crisis stems from a loss of integrity? I don't think so. In fact, the titles on that book table included several volumes that highlighted the need for character, decency, honor, and ethics. People certainly seem to have at least a vague notion that character issues lie at the heart of the leadership crisis.

The problem is that we live in an era where the very definition of *character* has become fuzzy. People bemoan the loss of integrity in general terms, but few have any clear idea of what "integrity" entails anymore. Moral standards have been systematically obliterated. Ours is the first society since the decaying Roman Empire to normalize homosexuality. We're living in the first generation in hundreds of years that has legalized abortion. Adultery and divorce are epidemic. Pornography is now an enormous industry and a major blight on the moral character of society. Virtually no clear moral or ethical standards are universally accepted anymore. No wonder principled, uncompromising personal integrity is hard to find.

But I'm optimistic. I'm convinced this is an era of unprecedented opportunity for the church—if we'll take advantage of it. The leadership vacuum is screaming to be filled. If godly men and women will step out and *lead*, people are prepared to follow the right kind of example. Hostile times and adverse circumstances are no impediment to a true leader. In fact, great adversity can be turned to great advantage by the power of an influential leader.

We see an illustration of that truth, in microcosm, in the apostle Paul's experience in Acts 27.

If you want a human model of leadership, I don't think you'll ever find a better model than Paul. Paul is my hero as a leader. He was a true leader of people, and his leadership rose to the occasion in every conceivable situation. His leadership abilities had nothing to do with titles. He wasn't governor of any territory; he wasn't the commander of any troops; he wasn't a nobleman of any kind. God had conferred on him the title of apostle, but that was his *only* title, and it had no relevance outside the church. Yet in Acts 27, we see him taking charge of a situation in a hostile secular environment when other men—powerful men—proved unable to lead.

Paul was not (especially in this situation) a man of high position. He was, however, a man of great influence—a natural leader.

What we find in Acts 27 is a very interesting situation. Paul was beginning the long journey from Caesarea to Rome, where he would be tried in the court of Caesar. He was to be transported in chains as a prisoner.

PAUL IN CAESAREA

Caesarea was the main Roman military outpost on the coast of Israel, directly west of Jerusalem and slightly north of the modern city of Tel Aviv. It was the chief port and jumping-off point for Roman officials during the

Roman occupation of Israel. It was also the capital of the Judean province and home to the Roman procurators. This was where Pilate lived during the time of Christ. It was completely Roman in culture.

The apostle Paul had been brought to Caesarea as a prisoner. His life as a missionary and church planter appeared to be over. When he returned from his third missionary journey in Acts 21:15, he returned to Jerusalem. He had collected money from Gentile churches all over Asia to give to the church at Jerusalem because the needs of that church were so great.

In Acts 21:11, the prophet Agabus had warned Paul that in Jerusalem he would be taken prisoner by the Jews and handed over to the Gentiles. Paul knew the prophecy was true, but he was committed to the ministry God had called him to, and he replied, "I am ready not only to be bound, but also to die at Jerusalem for the name of the Lord Jesus" (v. 13).

According to Acts 21:27, Paul went to the temple in Jerusalem, where he was seen by some Jewish worshipers from Asia who recognized him. They falsely accused him of defiling the temple. They knew he was traveling with Trophimus, who was a Gentile, and Acts 21:29 says they falsely supposed Paul had brought Trophimus with him into the temple—which was forbidden for Gentiles. So they started a great riot over what began as a simple misunderstanding born out of their hatred for Paul.

Paul was therefore arrested and taken to Caesarea for trial. Apparently, the Romans didn't know what to do with him. They seem to have arrested him mainly to pacify the Jewish leaders who were screaming for vengeance against him. Paul was then kept in custody in Caesarea for more than two years (Acts 24:27). He was put on trial first before Felix, then before Festus, then before Herod Agrippa II. Two Roman governors and the last ruler in the Herodian dynasty all personally heard his case. Each one judged him unworthy of death or chains, but they kept him in prison anyway, because to release him would have created political problems with the Jewish leaders in Jerusalem.

It was during the trial before Festus that Paul appealed directly to Caesar. This was his right as a Roman citizen. According to Acts 26:32,

Agrippa privately told Festus, "This man might have been set free if he had not appealed to Caesar" (Acts 26:32). Perhaps he really meant that. More likely, Herod and Festus would have continued using Paul as a pawn. But since Paul had appealed to Nero, he had to be sent to Rome.

That is the historical context at the beginning of Acts 27. Paul is in Caesarea. He is to be sent to Rome to stand trial before Nero. His long imprisonment in Caesarea is over, and now a new chapter begins as the Roman procurator makes arrangements for the long passage to Rome.

PAUL IN CUSTODY

At this point, the narrative of the book of Acts shifts gears. Luke begins writing in first person, suggesting that he was permitted to go along as Paul's companion on the journey to Rome. So what he writes is his own firsthand testimony—an inspired eyewitness chronicle. And he begins to color in more details. In fact, this chapter of Acts is said by some scholars to contain more information about ancient seafaring than virtually any other first-century source. And, amazingly, there are more words in Scripture devoted to detailing Paul's journey from Caesarea to Rome than all the words about creation in Genesis. So it is an important account.

When the journey to Rome began, Paul was clearly the low man on the totem pole. He had no authority. He had no responsibility. He had no rights. As a prisoner, he was at the bottom, both physically and socially.

I've spent some time ministering in prisons. In fact, I recently visited a prison where some well-known men are incarcerated. One of them used to be president of one of the largest life insurance companies in America. Another was a famous building contractor who had earned millions before losing it all in some kind of fraud scandal. There were several formidable people in that prison—people who were accustomed to power, men who knew what it was to wield authority. Mixed in with them was the usual assortment of drug dealers, neo-Nazi members of the Aryan Brotherhood, and various street criminals.

You know what I noticed? No one had a DayTimer. None of them had cell phones, secretaries, pin-striped suits, or silk ties. They had been stripped of all the accoutrements of power. They were told when to get up, when to eat, when to exercise, and when to work in the laundry. No one had any authority.

In fact, I had taken a Bible to give to a certain inmate, but I was told he wasn't allowed to have it. The only way I could get it to him was through the designated prison chaplain, and the chaplain first was required to tear off the book's front and back covers so that no prisoner could use the hard cover boards to make weapons.

Prisoners have no authority. That was Paul's situation. Undoubtedly, the ship he was to sail on was selected for him by Roman officials. He was placed in the company of a man named Julius, whom Luke says was "a centurion of the Augustan Regiment" (Acts 27:1)—an imperial cohort. As a centurion, Julius had a hundred men under his command, and they were specifically assigned to work for Caesar. So as centurions go, he was one of the highest ranking in the entire Roman army, and his men would have been elite soldiers.

By the way, here's an interesting footnote: Every time you encounter a Roman centurion in Scripture, you find a man of integrity—a respectable, intelligent, virtuous man. The Romans were not very good at selecting governors, but apparently they had some means of choosing their centurions that weeded out the weak and incompetent. We meet centurions in Matthew 8 and Luke 7, Mark 15, Acts 10, Acts 22, and Acts 24, and all of them are upright men of decency and honor. Julius is no exception to the rule.

Luke wrote, "So, entering a ship of Adramyttium, we put to sea, meaning to sail along the coasts of Asia" (Acts 27:2). The plan was for Julius to ride this ship with Paul toward Adramyttium, and at some major port along the way, they would pick up another ship to Rome.

The verse concludes: "Aristarchus, a Macedonian of Thessalonica, was with us." Aristarchus was a friend and companion of Luke and Paul. He is mentioned in Acts 20:4 as one of several members of the Thessalonian church who accompanied Paul home to Jerusalem after his third missionary journey. According to Acts 19:29, Aristarchus was also with Paul in Ephesus when that whole city rioted at the preaching of the gospel. So he had been a longtime friend and companion of Paul's—no doubt a believer and a fellow minister. He had apparently stayed with Paul through those years of imprisonment at Caesarea. Now he would accompany Paul and Luke on their trip to Rome.

That sets the scene. Paul is a prisoner. The ship would have a captain and probably a first mate. Under them would be other ranking sailors. Overseeing Paul's custody was a Roman centurion, and verses 31–32 say he had some of his soldiers with him—crack troops. So there were a lot of people with authority on that ship.

Not Paul. He was at the bottom of everything—perhaps even in the literal sense. He would no doubt have been kept in the hold of the ship.

PAUL AT LIBERTY

But Julius seems to have been a noble man, and Acts 27:3 says after just one day's travel, during the first stop, at Sidon, on the very first day of the trip, some seventy miles north on the Mediterranean coast from Caesarea, he "treated Paul kindly and gave him liberty to go to his friends and receive care."

The expression translated "receive care" is a medical term. It indicates that the apostle Paul was probably suffering from some kind of ailment. That isn't any wonder, since he had been a prisoner for so long. Of course, Luke was a physician (Colossians 4:14), and one of his duties, no doubt, was to care for Paul. But something about his ailment warranted a visit ashore. He would not have been able to gain the diet, the rest, and the care he needed while remaining onboard ship. So Julius granted Paul shore leave to be cared for by friends. They ministered to his physical needs, and Paul no doubt ministered to their spiritual needs.

That was certainly unusual. Julius might have sent one or more soldiers to accompany Paul and his band. But for a hot-potato political prisoner like Paul to be given even that much liberty was highly irregular. After all, Paul had stood before the governor Felix, the governor Festus, and King Agrippa. He had been deemed a serious enough threat to the *Pax Romana*—the peace of the Roman Empire—that he had been kept prisoner for more than two years. He was blamed for riots in the city of Jerusalem. The actual charge brought against him before Felix was that he was "a pestilent fellow" (Acts 24:5 KJV). He was "a plague, a creator of dissension among all the Jews throughout the world, and a ringleader of the sect of the Nazarenes" (v. 5). His case was now to come before Caesar.

You don't just give that kind of prisoner liberty without good reason. If a Roman soldier ever lost a prisoner because of negligence, he paid with his life. That fact comes into play later in Luke's account (27: 42–43). And yet here, Julius gave Paul permission to visit friends at Sidon and receive care from them.

Julius was a top Roman centurion. He was a highly trained soldier—a tough, seasoned fighter with the skills of a commander and the mental attitude of a sergeant. Why would he let a prisoner have liberty after he had been in his custody only one day?

There is only one reason: he trusted him.

Here is the first principle of leadership: *A leader is trustworthy.*

Somehow, either while still a prisoner in Caesarea, or in the one day's journey—or, likely, both—Paul had caused that centurion to believe that he would never do anything that would cost the centurion personally. Julius was convinced Paul would not take the liberty he gave and try to escape. So he let him go to his friends.

It seems Paul had friends everywhere. Of course, he had enemies everywhere too. But he had some friends in Sidon who no doubt had benefited from the influence of Paul's ministry over the years. He must have *asked* the centurion for permission to visit those friends. And the centurion let him visit them. He obviously had no fear in giving Paul this unusual degree of liberty and even put him in the hands of a group that could, if they were so inclined, try to help effect his escape.

How did Paul earn Julius's trust so quickly? Scripture doesn't say. Paul was obviously a gracious, godly man. His personal integrity ran deep. It is possible that the governor, Festus, who knew Paul's innocence, had assured Julius that Paul could be trusted, and ordered him to treat him courteously.

That this trust had developed is indicated in Acts 24:23, because what the centurion did is precisely what the previous governor, Felix, did: "He commanded the centurion to keep Paul and to let him have liberty, and told him not to forbid any of his friends to provide for or visit him." All this is clear evidence that Paul had earned a reputation of trust. Even the governors under whom he was imprisoned knew he was a man of integrity. And somehow that trust was communicated to Julius.

Julius could also surely see that Paul's companions, Luke and Aristarchus, were devoted to him. They hadn't abandoned him when he was imprisoned. On the contrary, they were willing to accompany him all the way to Rome, at great personal risk to their own lives. Let's face it: this was not like taking a cruise to Honolulu on a luxury liner. This was a small, clumsy, inhospitable Roman sailing vessel. Quarters were tight and uncomfortable. Moreover, some historians believe the only way Luke and Aristarchus would have been permitted to accompany Paul on this trip was if they went as slaves. Whatever the terms of their travel, you can be sure the Roman govern-ment did not pay their fare. No

> *Leadership Principle #1*
> A LEADER IS TRUSTWORTHY.

matter what circumstances opened the door for them to accompany Paul, it was a major personal sacrifice for Luke and Aristarchus. But they did it because of their love for the apostle. They were clearly committed to him.

Paul's friends in Sidon also obviously trusted him. They opened their home to him, even though he was a prisoner. Rather than seeing his captivity as casting doubt on his integrity, they welcomed him and refreshed him. No one inspires such devotion without being trustworthy.

Paul also certainly would have treated Julius with the utmost respect. He also must have conversed with him, shown an interest in him, and quickly developed a liking for Julius, and Julius returned that respect. Therefore by the time they were one day into their journey, Julius already trusted Paul enough to give him liberty.

How does a leader build trust? When people are convinced you will do everything in your power for their good and nothing for their harm, they'll trust you. This centurion obviously was convinced that Paul honestly had his best interests at heart, so he gave him a measure of freedom. He clearly had a high degree of confidence that Paul would not try to escape. If Julius had the slightest concern about whether Paul would come back to the ship voluntarily, he would have kept him under guard on the ship. But Paul had gained his trust. All leadership begins there.

Paul cared about that man. He was aware of Julius's duty, sensitive to his concerns, and he would not have done anything to discredit or dishonor him, much less jeopardize his life. Thus the power of Paul's character influenced Julius. Paul, the prisoner, was in effect "leading" Julius, his captor.

A leader is not someone who is consumed with his own success and his own best interests. A *true* leader is someone who demonstrates to everyone around him that their interests are what most occupy his heart. A real leader will work hard to make everyone around him successful. His passion is to help make the people under his leadership flourish. That is *why* a true leader must have the heart of a servant.

A person cannot be a true leader and operate only for personal fulfillment or personal gain. People whose motives are selfish end up leading nobody, because everyone abandons them. They cannot be trusted. A person in a position of leadership will succeed only as long as people trust him with their futures, with their money, or even with their lives. Nothing can take the place of trust. Nothing. A leader you can't trust is no true leader at all. He may be a man in power who can force people to do what he wants, but he is no example of true leadership.

Here's how you can easily recognize genuine leaders: They are the ones surrounded by gifted, capable, diligent, effective people who are devoted to their leader. That devotion reflects *trust*. And trust stems from the selfless way the godly leader uses his own energies and his own abilities in a sacrificial, selfless way. If you can show people you truly have *their* best interests at heart, they'll follow you.

This man was so convinced that Paul would never do anything to bring him harm that he let him go to his friends.

And, of course, Paul came back. He proved himself worthy of Julius's trust. Paul was thereby building *more* trust that would further strengthen his own hand for leadership later in the journey.

Chapter Two

TAKING THE INITIATIVE

When Paul's long journey to Rome got under way again after that brief stop in Sidon, the ship encountered what would be the bane of the whole trip: contrary winds. Luke wrote: "When we had put to sea from [Sidon], we sailed under the shelter of Cyprus, because the winds were contrary. And when we had sailed over the sea which is off Cilicia and Pamphylia, we came to Myra, a city of Lycia" (Acts 27:4–5).

THE GOING GETS TOUGH

In order to see how Paul's leadership lifts him even higher among the men on the ship, until he is completely in charge and everyone is dependent on him, we need to look into the details of this story.

Cyprus is an island just south of Asia Minor, north and west of the land of Israel (see map). Myra is a harbor town a little farther west and just on the southern tip of Asia Minor, in modern-day Turkey. So after leaving Sidon, on the northern coast of modern-day Lebanon, the ship's captain turned west toward Rome and sailed northwesterly in the direction of his home port, Adramyttium. Cyprus was the closest island, and a large one. The winds were from the west, so they sailed to the east of Cyprus, trying to avoid the stiff winds as much as possible.

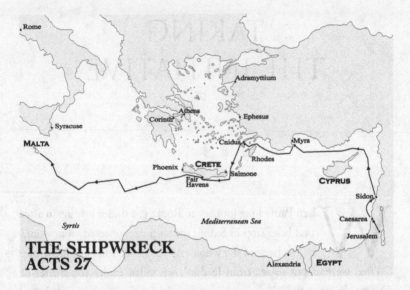

**THE SHIPWRECK
ACTS 27**

Obviously, a sailing vessel cannot sail straight into a strong wind. The only way to advance into headwinds is by a maneuver called *tacking*. Tacking involves steering a zigzag course, first perpendicular to the wind, utilizing the sails to gain speed, then turning into the wind and dropping the sails to allow the ship's momentum to carry it into the wind. Then the sails are raised at the opportune moment and the ship runs perpendicular to the wind again. The maneuver is extremely difficult and labor-intensive, but it makes it possible to sail into a moderate headwind.

There were several kinds of ships in those days. Some were large ships that ventured into the open sea to transport loads of cargo through the shipping lanes. Others were port hoppers that skidded along near the coastlines and moved from port to port. This was apparently a ship of the second variety, because Luke describes its journey from port to port. It went from Caesarea to Sidon, then from Sidon to Myra, on the southern tip of Asia Minor.

The route was somewhat out of the way for a journey to Rome. It would have been a straight shot west from Sidon to Rhodes (nearly halfway to Rome). But because of the winds, instead of sailing straight for Rhodes, they made a detour that took them north of Cyprus, a safer but less direct route.

The chronological clues in Acts suggest that it was mid-August, which is consistent with what we know about the wind patterns of the region. In August, the winds are westerly.

Sailing season was quickly coming to an end. From approximately November 11 to the end of March, winter winds on the Mediterranean can be treacherous, so no ships made any regular crossings during those months. And even in early autumn, from September 14 to November 11, travel on the Mediterranean could be risky. So time was short to make the journey, and speed was of the essence. According to maritime historians, the journey from Sidon to Myra, into a headwind, would have taken approximately nine days. By the time Paul and his entourage arrived at Myra, the dangerous season was already approaching.

Myra had a harbor. The city itself was some two miles inland, but the harbor was a busy, active port, chiefly for vessels from Egypt.

Egypt was a major source of grain for the Roman Empire. Ships would bring grain from Egypt to the granaries of Myra, offload, and return to Egypt. Other ships bound for Rome would collect the grain and carry it to the imperial capital. There happened to be in Myra one of these ships bound for Italy. Luke said, "There the centurion found an Alexandrian ship sailing to Italy, and he put us on board" (Acts 27:6).

This second ship, we discover, was a large one and more seaworthy than the first ship, capable of carrying 276 passengers in addition to its heavy cargo. The ship was registered in Alexandria, which is in Egypt. So it was undoubtedly one of the grain transport vessels. Since it was already late in the year to be crossing the Mediterranean, they apparently wasted no time at Myra. They began the journey to Rome immediately.

Verse 7 says, "When we had sailed slowly many days, and arrived with difficulty off Cnidus, the wind not permitting us to proceed, we sailed under the shelter of Crete off Salmone."

The westerly winds were apparently increasing in intensity. It was becoming difficult to tack and make progress. From Luke's description, we can discern the route they took. They followed the inside passage between Rhodes and the mainland of Asia Minor. This took them farther west and a little bit farther north. Cnidus was a city on a small island at the tip of a long peninsula. It marks the southwestern extremity of Asia Minor, just north of Rhodes. The island was connected to the mainland by an artificial causeway, which gave the city two ports, one north of the causeway and the other south.

Paul's ship normally would have made port in one of the harbors there. But as they approached Cnidus, their route took them into open sea. There they lost the advantage of the gentle offshore winds. They plunged right into the prevailing wind and the pummeling headwaters. The wind in the open sea turned out to be so powerful that they could not direct the ship into harbor at Cnidus.

At that point, they had no choice but to sail south, toward the island of Crete. The plan was to sail along the southern coast of Crete, where they would be somewhat protected from the powerful winds, and turn into a safe harbor there.

They sailed past Salmone, a promontory, or cape, on the northeastern corner of Crete. Luke implied that the weather was already worsening: "Passing [Salmone] with difficulty, we came to a place called Fair Havens, near the city of Lasea" (v. 8). The brevity of Luke's words camouflage the degree of difficulty they would have experienced. Crete is approximately 170 miles long and only 35 miles wide at its widest point. From Salmone to Fair Havens was at least 140 miles. So the expression "great difficulty" is surely an understatement.

The name of Fair Havens, however, was an overstatement. It was a small port, consisting of an open bay, sheltered by only two small islands. Luke said, "The harbor was not suitable to winter in" (v. 12). The nearby town of Lasea was small, so it may have been that supplies and accommodations were sparse. But perhaps more important, the captain of the ship would have been eager to get to Rome and sell his cargo. To winter in Fair Havens would have meant a four-month delay, and the ship's owner would have to pay the crew's wages and buy their supplies during that time. From an economic point of view, a winter in Fair Havens would have been disastrous.

Apparently, however, the ship was unavoidably delayed in this port—perhaps by the weather, or perhaps by the difficulty of getting supplies. Luke said, "Much time had been spent, and sailing was now dangerous because the Fast was already over" (v. 9). "The Fast" is a reference to the Day of Atonement, Yom Kippur. That is the tenth day of the seventh month on the Jewish calendar, which would make it close to the beginning of October. Crossing the open sea at that time of year was a very dangerous proposition. It was like gambling with one's life.

But it was a gamble the sailors were prepared to take. They wanted to get their vessel out of Fair Havens, and they thought they could winter better at a port called Phoenix. This was on the west coast of Crete. It had a semicircular harbor with openings on the southwest and northwest, and it was more protected against the harsh winter winds. So their plan was to sail along the coast of Crete until they reached that port.

Paul could see what was coming. He knew it was a risky and foolhardy plan. He had been in at least three shipwrecks before this (cf. 2 Corinthians 11:25, which was written a few years prior to this episode), and he was obviously not eager to suffer through another one. Luke said, "Paul advised them, saying, 'Men, I perceive that this voyage will end with disaster and much loss, not only of the cargo and ship, but also our lives'" (vv. 9–10).

"Paul advised them"? Don't miss the significance of that statement. Who was Paul to advise these sailors? He was a prisoner. What's happening here?

This is a second foundational principle of true leadership: *A leader takes the initiative.*

This ship was loaded with powerful men. There were the captain, his pilot, and other ranking sailors. There were a centurion and other Roman soldiers from an imperial regiment. All of them would have undoubtedly had strong opinions about whether or not to leave Fair Havens. They were no doubt all dissatisfied with the delay and eager to get moving toward their destination. They had surely discussed all the possibilities. They were aware that the trip would be dangerous, and that the danger increased the longer they waited.

All of them had a formal right to speak, and to render an opinion about the advisability of the journey. Much was at stake for all of them. The soldiers who had Paul in custody obviously wanted to get to Rome as fast as they could. The ship's owners and crew wanted to get their cargo to Italy as rapidly as they could, because it meant money to them. Almost everyone had good reason to want to keep moving.

But it was Paul who seized the initiative and spoke out. He recognized the danger and pointed it out clearly. He had no rank. He had no particular right. He had no title. He had no authority. But he realized there was a problem, so he took the initiative and tried to bring clarity to the situation. That's leadership. Leaders rise in times of crisis by taking the initiative.

THE TOUGH GET GOING

Paul's instincts and his judgment were correct, as subsequent events would show. As Luke recounts the story, it seems that while everyone else was still analyzing the situation, Paul already had it sized up. So he spoke out.

That is a vital mark of true leadership. A leader never says, "We might have a problem over here. Somebody ought to do something about it." The leader says, "Here is the problem, and here's how to solve it."

Another classic biblical example of a leader who took the initiative was Nehemiah. Almost five hundred years before Paul, while the nation of Israel was just emerging from a long time of captivity in a foreign land,

Nehemiah single-handedly united the people of Jerusalem and rebuilt the walls of that city in fifty-two days' time. It was one of the most remarkable displays of strategic initiative and courageous leadership ever recorded in history. Though it takes us from the New Testament to the Old Testament, Nehemiah's example is worth our attention, because he provides us with a rich and vivid case study that highlights this core feature of leadership.

Nehemiah was nobody very special as far as the people of Jerusalem

> *Leadership Principle #2*
> **A LEADER TAKES THE INITIATIVE.**

were concerned. He was a servant in the palace of the king of Persia. The captivity had been over for some eighty years, but Nehemiah had remained in Persia as a servant. He had never even visited his homeland. He first learned of the ruined condition of Jerusalem from his brother, who returned from a visit to Jerusalem and reported what he had seen: "The survivors who are left from the captivity in the province are there in great distress and reproach. The wall of Jerusalem is also broken down, and its gates are burned with fire" (Nehemiah 1:3).

That sparked something in Nehemiah that unleashed his leadership ability. He decided on the spot that he was going to take the initiative and rebuild those walls.

It would have been easy for Nehemiah to ignore the problem. After all, he lived more than 750 miles from Jerusalem. He might have simply basked in the comforts of the king's palace, feeling sorry about the state of his homeland and wishing someone would organize a plan to remedy the situation.

But that's not what leaders do. They take the initiative. They rise up and build.

A WISE MASTER BUILDER

The way Nehemiah took up his calling makes a superb study in how true leaders take the initiative. This will be almost as much of a detour as the route the apostle Paul's ship took on his journey to Rome, but there is much to learn from the digression. So let's leave Paul and his companions at Fair Havens for the moment, and recall how Nehemiah led the efforts to rebuild Jerusalem's walls:

First, He Identified the Problem

From the moment Nehemiah learned that Jerusalem was still in ruins, he saw precisely what it meant, and he prayerfully rehearsed the situation in prayer before the throne of God. He wrote, "So it was, when I heard these words, that I sat down and wept, and mourned for many days; I was fasting and praying before the God of heaven" (Nehemiah 1:4).

The problem was not that God was unfaithful; but rather that His people had been unfaithful. They had broken the covenant. Nehemiah began his prayer by acknowledging God's faithfulness: "I said: 'I pray, LORD God of heaven, O great and awesome God, You who keep Your covenant and mercy with those who love You and observe Your commandments'" (v. 5).

And then he identified the real problem: "Please let Your ear be attentive and Your eyes open, that You may hear the prayer of Your servant which I pray before You now, day and night, for the children of Israel Your servants, and confess the sins of the children of Israel which *we have sinned against You. Both my father's house and I have sinned. We have acted very corruptly against You, and have not kept the commandments, the statutes, nor the ordinances which You commanded Your servant Moses*" (vv. 6–7, emphasis added). He then rehearsed God's promise of forgiveness and restoration, and begged God to use him to bring about the restoration of Jerusalem.

Then He Came Up with a Solution

It is obvious from Nehemiah's prayer and his subsequent actions that he was already formulating a plan. At the end of his prayer in Nehemiah 1:11, he prayed, "Let Your servant prosper this day, I pray, and grant him mercy in the sight of this man."

"This man" is a reference to the king of Persia, Artaxerxes. Nehemiah had decided to petition the king—at the risk of his own life—for permission to return to Jerusalem and organize the rebuilding of the walls.

The extent of Nehemiah's planning became obvious when he sought the king's assistance. The king's only questions to Nehemiah were: "How long will your journey be? And when will you return?" Nehemiah obviously already knew how long the task would require, because he said, "I set him a time" (2:6).

Furthermore, Nehemiah had other specific requests: "I said to the king, 'If it pleases the king, let letters be given to me for the governors of the region beyond the River, that they must permit me to pass through till I come to Judah, and a letter to Asaph the keeper of the king's forest, that he must give me timber to make beams for the gates of the citadel which pertains to the temple, for the city wall, and for the house that I will occupy'" (vv. 7–8). He had done careful calculations. He knew how much lumber he would need for beams and scaffolds and housing. He anticipated the problems he might face, and therefore he asked for letters of conveyance. He already had a strategy in place.

This was all the more remarkable when we remember that Nehemiah was no stonemason. He wasn't a building contractor. He was a domestic servant—a butler to the king. He had no particular occupational skills that would have qualified him to oversee a project on such an immense scale as the rebuilding of a city's walls.

But he knew how to identify and solve problems. He was a careful planner. He thought through the whole venture, anticipated the difficulties, and worked out solutions in advance. He wasn't winging it. He wasn't making things up on the fly as he went along. He had carefully counted the cost. He had a well-formulated plan, and he stuck to it. All this flowed from his willingness to take the initiative.

The genius of Nehemiah's plan became evident as the work on the walls got under way. Nehemiah 3 is a chronicle of the names of all the people who worked on the wall. And Nehemiah's skill as an organizer shines through that chapter. He divided the entire city wall into small, manageable portions and put key people in charge of each section. Everyone shared in the work, and everyone had a well-defined, achievable task. That is how Nehemiah managed to finish the task in such a remarkably short time.

Furthermore, Nehemiah illustrates that effective initiative is not short-lived. It runs to the end of the necessity until all bases are covered and the objective is achieved. This is a far cry from the common idea of people who think they have the answer to the dilemma but cannot ride that initiative from the initial idea to its fulfillment. The only kind of starting power that makes true leaders is that which not only starts the ignition, but also drives to the end of the journey, organizing and mobilizing people along the way.

We see that, too, in Nehemiah. Notice that he knew his workers. He listed them by name and recorded precisely what section of the wall each one built (Nehemiah 3). He remained committed to the project and inti-mately involved in every phase of it until it was brought to completion.

He Delegated Responsibility

Nonetheless, Nehemiah did not take the responsibility of oversight and labor for the entire wall upon himself. He appointed trustworthy men to oversee sections of the labor, dividing their responsibilities in accord with their abilities.

This was the only way to accomplish the rebuilding of Jerusalem's walls in so short a time. It was a team effort—or rather, the combined effort of multiple teams. That way Nehemiah was able to employ the maxi-mum number of workers and get the most out of them.

Furthermore, he shrewdly assigned people to work at locations close to their own homes. The priests built the section closest to the Temple (3:1). "Jedaiah the son of Harumaph made repairs in front of his house" (v. 10). "Hashabiah, leader of half the district of Keilah, made repairs for his district" (v. 17). "Benjamin and Hasshub made repairs opposite their house. After them Azariah the son of Maaseiah, the son of Ananiah, made repairs by his house" (v. 23). "Meshullam the son of Berechiah made repairs in front of his dwelling" (v. 30). And so on. This gave each team an extra incentive to do excellent work. No one would want the part of the wall next to his own house to be weak or sloppy looking.

It was a wise plan that made the most of each man's labor. It guaranteed that they would take pride in their work. And it assured that they would finish their assigned tasks.

He Knew How to Motivate People

When Nehemiah first arrived in Jerusalem, the captivity had already been over for a full century. Jews had been returning to the land in waves, starting with Zerubbabel in 538 BC. The first job undertaken by the first returnees was the rebuilding of the temple. The Old Testament book of Ezra records what an ordeal that was. After the foundation was laid in 536, the temple remained unfinished for some twenty-one years. It was finally completed at the urging of Haggai and Zechariah, in 515. Nehemiah arrived in Jerusalem seventy-one years later, in 414 BC.

No one in all those years had taken the initiative to complete the rebuilding of the city. The first sight that greeted every visitor was the ruined wall. Massive piles of rubble surrounded the city, mute testimony to the divine judgment that had overthrown Judea and carried her people into captivity. It was an embarrassment as well as a hazard. But a hundred years had passed and no one had even suggested a rebuilding project.

Isn't it remarkable that Nehemiah, a newcomer to the city, could gather the people together, challenge them to rebuild the walls, and get an immediate positive response: "Let us rise up and build" (Nehemiah 2:18)?

Nehemiah obviously knew what it takes to motivate people. He did not do it by sheer hype, manipulation, or theatrics. But he shared his vision in a way the people could grasp. He explained how the goal was attainable. And, in Nehemiah's own words, "I told them of the hand of my God which had been good upon me, and also of the king's words that he had spoken to me" (2:18). He helped them to see that this was a work of God. He showed them the spiritual importance of it. He was sincere and believable. His enthusiasm was infectious. His optimism was contagious. They caught the vision.

He Worked Alongside the People

Nehemiah was not a *passive* leader. Good leaders never are. They don't ask others to do what they are unwilling to do themselves. Nehemiah rolled up his sleeves and worked as diligently as anyone else. "We labored in the work," Nehemiah said (4:21). He wasn't afraid to get his own hands dirty.

In fact, as Nehemiah described the work, he put in long days of non-stop toil until the task was complete: "Neither I, my brethren, my servants, nor the men of the guard who followed me took off our clothes, except that everyone took them off for washing" (4:23). He said in Nehemiah 5:16, "Indeed, I also continued the work on this wall, and we did not buy any land." All his other business was put on hold while he worked.

He was relentless. He was dedicated to the work. And the people of Jerusalem followed his lead against ridicule, conspiracy, discouragement, deceit, and every form of vicious opposition. Chapters 4 through 6 of his account record in detail how Nehemiah's enemies desperately tried to stop his work.

And in spite of all of that, because of the initiative of this one man, the entire wall around Jerusalem was completed in just fifty-two days' time (6:15).

Nehemiah was the epitome of an effective leader. He was a starter. He was strongly motivated. He knew how to organize and motivate followers. He overcame obstacles. He was practical and wise and determined. He was a man of action, but thoughtful, too. All those qualities are essential to effective leadership. Combined, they made Nehemiah the kind of man—like the apostle Paul—who was not afraid to take initiative. And therein lay the secret of both men's success.

INTO THE TEMPEST

Meanwhile, back in Fair Havens, the soldiers and sailors discussed Paul's advice and decided to reject it. Luke wrote, "Nevertheless the centurion was more persuaded by the helmsman and the owner of the ship than by the things spoken by Paul. And because the harbor was not suitable to winter in, the majority advised to set sail from there also, if by any means they could reach Phoenix, a harbor of Crete opening toward the southwest and northwest, and winter there" (Acts 27:11–12).

In what seems an unusual, and utterly desperate, deviation from the norm, the captain of the ship seems to have solicited the will of "the majority." Most were in favor of trying to reach a more advantageous harbor. Give me one great, careful, thoughtful, analytical, wise leader over the majority *anytime*. But in this case, they took a vote. The ship's captain let an opinion poll make the decision for him.

Notice that the decision was made for purely pragmatic reasons. No one wanted to stay at Fair Havens. They were motivated by expediency and selfish desire, not by wisdom.

Here is a third vital principle of leadership: *A leader uses good judgment.*

According to the world's view, a leader is a risk taker—a dice roller. Leaders *are* often called upon to take a certain amount of legitimate, calculated risk. But a good leader never makes a decision that is a pure gamble. Wise leaders don't wager with their people. They don't subject their people to unnecessary hazards. Paul's advice was good judgment. By spurning it, the crew and the soldiers were gambling with everyone's lives. They were literally casting their fate to the wind, trusting blind luck that everything would turn out okay. That is not wise leadership.

I often tell young pastors that the fastest way to lose people's trust is not by preaching a bad sermon. People will forgive that. The fastest way to lose credibility as a leader is to make a foolish decision that leads people down a blind alley or off

> **Leadership Principle #3**
> A LEADER USES GOOD JUDGMENT.

the end of a pier. Too many young men in ministry make impetuous and ill-considered decisions. They lead without looking where they are going. They don't count the cost. They aren't cautious enough. You might think that young leaders would make the mistake of being too timid, but in my experience, it is much more common for young men to fail because they are impetuous. They aren't sensitive. They don't seek wise counsel.

Good leaders are analytical. They understand when there's a calculated risk, but they carefully assess the risk and plan for contingencies. If disaster is looming and there's no way out, they don't press ahead.

Much was in jeopardy with this decision to sail. The cargo, the ship, and the lives of all on board could be lost. That was precisely how Paul outlined the danger in verse 10.

Remember, "the centurion was more persuaded by the helmsman and the owner of the ship than by the things spoken by Paul" (v. 11). All of them wanted to get moving. And after all, why listen to Paul? What did *he* know about sailing the Mediterranean on a vessel like this? Thus the sole voice of wisdom was silenced.

They worked out a solution. It was only a relatively short distance— only about forty miles around the western end of Crete—to Phoenix. Phoenix was a better port than Fair Havens. It had a semicircular harbor with openings on the southwest and northwest, and it was more protected against the harsh winter winds. Perhaps they could at least get that far, and then decide whether to stay the winter or move on.

At first the winds seemed favorable. "When the south wind blew softly, supposing that they had obtained their desire, putting out to sea, they sailed close by Crete" (v. 13). A gentle south wind would have been warm, coming up from North Africa. The day looked pleasant enough as they set out to sea, sailing close by the southern coast of Crete.

It didn't last long. Luke said, "But not long after, a tempestuous head wind arose, called Euroclydon" (v. 14). This was a fierce wind from the northeast. It comes off the mountains above Lebanon and blows the cold winter air in hard blasts across the Mediterranean Sea. It was exactly what Paul had predicted would happen. The wisdom of his counsel was now obvious to all.

It became impossible to turn the ship north toward Phoenix, and the tempest was so powerful that they abandoned that as an option. Luke wrote, "So when the ship was caught, and could not head into the wind, we let her drive. And running under the shelter of an island called Clauda, we secured the skiff with difficulty" (vv. 15–16).

They were now about twenty-five miles off Crete, at the mercy of the wind. Clauda was a small island off the southwestern extremity of Crete. The "skiff" was a wooden dinghy towed by the ship. It was used to do maintenance on the hull and anchors, and in port it served as a tender, shuttling passengers back and forth to shore. (It was the only means they had to get safely to shore when they were anchored in a harbor.) It could also serve as a lifeboat, though it would not have been large enough to hold more than a few of the passengers. Apparently in the high winds, the skiff was being battered and was in danger of being lost.

So they secured the skiff by hauling it up onto the deck. Luke himself apparently helped do this, as indicated by his use of the pronoun *we*. The skiff was no doubt very heavy, and the high winds would have made the task more difficult. All hands were needed in such an emergency.

The ship itself was in danger of breaking up. Luke wrote, "When they had taken it on board, they used cables to undergird the ship" (v. 17). This was a procedure known as "frapping." The hulls of ships in those days were assembled with tongue-and-groove construction and sealed with pitch. In crashing waves, the slats would be under tremendous stress, and in danger of coming apart at crucial points. So cables—actually very large ropes—were passed under the ship and winched together on deck to hold the hull together.

An equally grave danger was the possibility that they might be blown off course and run aground. So, "fearing lest they should run aground on the Syrtis Sands, they struck sail and so were driven" (v. 17). The Syrtis Sands were a graveyard for ships in the Gulf of Sidra, off the African coast west of Cyrene. The water there was shallow, with hidden reefs and sandbanks. So "they struck sail," which means they took down the sail.

Luke wrote, "Because we were exceedingly tempest-tossed, the next day they lightened the ship. On the third day we threw the ship's tackle overboard with our own hands" (vv. 18–19). Everything Paul had warned them about was now coming to pass. Lightening the ship involved throwing the cargo overboard. The tackle was their equipment and tools. That was not a trivial thing, and the decision to do it would not have been made if they had not been in fear of their lives. The cargo and the tackle were their livelihood. But they jettisoned everything they could get their hands on to allow the ship to ride higher, so it wouldn't get swamped by the waves.

They had no means of navigation, and no way of knowing where they were. "When neither sun nor stars appeared for many days, and no small tempest beat on us, all hope that we would be saved was finally given up" (v. 20). They were resigned to the fact that they were going to die.

From a human standpoint, it seemed everything that could possibly go wrong had happened. The entire journey was unraveling into a major disaster. But behind the scenes, God was clearly in control. He had His chosen leader in place, ready to take charge, and in spite of the chaos of the situation, God planned to use it for good.

—

Chapter Three

TAKING COURAGE

W hen Luke described the storm as "no small tempest" in Acts 27:20, he was not kidding. Northeastern winds on the Mediterranean at that time of year are unpredictable, terrifying, and deadly. These were treacherous hurricane-force winds. They arose quickly and made it impossible to turn back to Fair Havens or to turn north toward Phoenix. Paul and his companions were at the mercy of the winds.

Thankfully, as Paul knew, "the LORD on high is mightier than the noise of many waters, than the mighty waves of the sea" (Psalm 93:4). "[He rules] the raging of the sea; when its waves rise, [He stills] them" (Psalm 89:9). "For He commands and raises the stormy wind, which lifts up the waves of the sea" (Psalm 107:25). God was still in sovereign control, even though from the sailors' vantage point, all looked hopeless.

What had started out as a forty-mile cruise along the coast turned into several days of sheer terror. Luke said both sun and stars were totally obscured "for many days" (v. 20). They had no way of knowing how far they had gone off course or where they were.

The terror of both passengers and crew was steadily intensifying. You can sense the panic growing. The day after the storm began, *"they* lightened the ship" (v. 18, emphasis added)—meaning, apparently, that the crew began to dump cargo. Some of the cargo was kept for ballast and essential supplies, but everything that could possibly be thrown overboard was jettisoned. We know this because Luke said, "On the third day *we* threw the ship's tackle overboard *with our own hands*" (v. 19, emphasis added). Luke himself—and very likely Paul as well—actually got involved in throwing things overboard. The picture Luke painted is that everything not nailed down was cast into the sea in a frenzied effort to further lighten the ship. Baggage, personal effects, the tools and equipment used by the sailors— everything that added weight—was thrown overboard. Their minds said the situation was hopeless, yet in desperation they fought to survive.

At this point the apostle Paul spoke up again . . .

"I *TOLD* YOU SO . . ."

Luke wrote, "After long abstinence from food, then Paul stood in the midst of them and said, 'Men, you should have listened to me, and not have sailed from Crete and incurred this disaster and loss'" (v. 21). Paul was human. He couldn't resist saying, "I told you so." Besides, he needed to remind them at this point of his earlier warning. The fact that he had been right before reinforced his credibility.

Notice that they hadn't eaten for days. This might be the result of three factors. First, in seas like that, even seasoned sailors get seasick. Most of them would not have even *wanted* to eat. Second, with seawater pouring into the ship's hold and cargo being jettisoned, it is likely that the majority of the fresh food supplies were spoiled. Third, and most practically, they were so busy trying to save the ship—running the frapping cables, tossing cargo overboard, making on-the-spot repairs, and doing all they could to stay afloat—they really had no time to eat. By then, all of them were thoroughly exhausted.

It might not have been the most receptive audience for an I-told-you-so lecture.

But there's much more to this than a finger-wagging scold. Paul was speaking up not merely to chide them, but to cheer them. His point was not to deride, but to encourage. Paul quickly made his intentions clear: "Now I urge you to take heart, for there will be no loss of life among you, but only of the ship" (v. 22). That's pretty strong confidence. Where did Paul get that confidence? He explained: "There stood by me this night an angel of the God to whom I belong and whom I serve, saying, 'Do not be afraid, Paul; you must be brought before Caesar; and indeed God has granted you all those who sail with you'" (vv. 23–24).

There's an irony in the angel's words of comfort to Paul. Paul was not to fear, because God's purpose was to bring him to the court of Caesar. The caesar in power at the time was Nero, an utter madman whose passionate and irrational hatred of Christians was legendary. Spurgeon said, "It seems no more comfort than if the angel had said, 'You can't be drowned, for you are to be devoured by a lion.'"[1]

Humanly speaking, there was every expectation that Paul would face a cruel death at the hands of the emperor. Ultimately, that is precisely what happened. By comparison, a drowning at sea might seem a much milder passage to heaven, and a welcome end to Paul's trials.

But Paul saw it as an opportunity to preach the gospel in Rome, in the court of Nero himself. This was what he had sought and prayed for, and even if it cost him his life, that was a price Paul was willing to pay to glorify Christ. Paul longed to "know [Christ] and the power of His resurrection, and the fellowship of His sufferings, being conformed to His death" (Philippians 3:10). For him, to live was Christ, and to die was gain (Philippians 1:21). He described himself as "hard-pressed between the two, having a desire to depart and be with Christ, which is far better" (1:23). His only desire was to glorify Christ in his death and take the gospel to Rome, to the very heart of his opposition, and proclaim the truth to Nero himself. Now he had an authoritative promise that he would be given that opportunity.

Here is a fourth characteristic of all wise leadership: *A leader speaks with authority.*

Paul had God's own promise of safety. He was confident it was true. He knew God was still in control of the winds, and that if God wanted Paul to testify before Caesar, a shipwreck would be no obstacle. Moreover, if God promised the safety of every soul on the ship, Paul could rest in the confidence that God would keep His word.

Therefore Paul was able to speak with the utmost boldness and conviction. His remarkable assurance was not born of *self*-confidence; it stemmed from the certainty that God would do as He said. "He cannot deny Himself" (2 Timothy 2:13).

Notice: When we say good leaders speak with authority, we're not merely saying that they speak with an authoritative attitude. Pomposity and arrogance aren't the same as authority. Paul's amazing aplomb was utterly devoid of anything like egotism or insolence. It did not reflect a feeling of superiority or a sense of self-importance and conceit. Rather, the amazing authority with which Paul spoke was an unshakable authority derived from his absolute certainty that God's Word was true and His promises were trustworthy.

Of course, there's no denying that there was a commanding air to the manner in which Paul seized the moment. He *did* speak definitively. He *did* sound certain and assertive. A true leader is able to speak with such boldness because he knows whereof he speaks. He speaks with confidence—with authority—because he knows what is true. He sees it plainly. In Paul's case, he stood on God's own authority. He had direct revelation from God!

And so do we. God has spoken clearly in His Word to us. Scripture is the very voice of God, alive and powerful—and for the believer, illuminated by the indwelling Holy Spirit. Scripture, said Paul, is "the mind of Christ" (1 Corinthians 2:16). It reveals what He thinks—and He thinks in perfect accord with the will of God, as does the Holy Spirit (Romans 8:26).

We can't expect angelic revelation, since that was unique to the apostolic era. They didn't have the New Testament. We do, and that is where God still speaks. Every leader who is a Christian has far more than any worldly leader, because we have God's truth and His Spirit as our teacher.

All of this means that a leader must *know* the Scriptures. He must *believe* with an unshakable conviction that God's Word is true. And he must be able to *communicate* the truth of God's Word with confidence and conviction.

Paul also under-stood that there *is* a vocal and verbal ele-

> *Leadership Principle #4*
> A LEADER SPEAKS WITH AUTHORITY.

ment to leadership that cannot be discounted. A few years ago, I spoke at the local police academy's graduation ceremony. Afterward, I was talking to a commander about how difficult it is to get through the academy. He told me about one student they dismissed from the academy because his voice was too soft and high-pitched. I expressed some surprise about that, but he pointed out that you can't come up behind someone and say with a voice like Mickey Mouse, "Put 'em up! You're under arrest!"

The voice of authority must convey strength and power. Unless you really know what you're talking about, you can't speak clearly or with authority. And if you can't verbally project certainty, confidence, and courage based on knowledge, you'll find it very difficult to lead people.

A leader doesn't say, "Well, we could go this way, or we could go that way. Let's *vote*." In the business world or the athletic world, the true leader is always the guy who pulls everyone into the huddle and says, "This is what we do. Here is how we do it. This is how we win." Then he lays out a clear and sensible plan and says, "Now, everyone, go do your job." He knows what he's talking about. He understands the problems. He sees the solutions. He communicates it all clearly so that everyone is motivated to do what's needed.

In the apostle Paul's case, he had a word from God. That is what sets spiritual and biblical leadership apart from every other kind. We can speak with absolute confidence, as long as we derive our authority from the unshakable truth of God's Word.

Despite what some who listen to my tapes might think, I don't speak with authority on *everything*. I've been invited many times to be a guest on *Larry King Live* or some other talk show to give my opinion. Sometimes I decline. When someone asks me my opinion about our government's economic or foreign-relations policies, I usually offer no opinion. I don't have enough valid information about those things to have an authoritative opinion. Ask me about some moral or ethical question, however, and that's another matter. Why? Because I know what Scripture says about those things. I have authority for my opinions on such matters. And when given the opportunity, I always point to my source of authority. I don't like giving *mere* opinion.

People are looking for authority they can trust. And people who love the truth will follow someone who communicates God's truth with authority. There's no need to tiptoe around facts, evade hard issues, or equivocate on clear matters. If you know the truth, speak it with authority! That's what true leadership does.

You wouldn't hear Jesus say, "I'd like to share something with you. I have a thought that might be worth your consideration." He amazed people by the way He spoke with authority. Of course, He had inherent authority, because He was God incarnate. But His manner of speaking contrasted starkly with that of the Scribes and Pharisees. Matthew said, "The people were astonished at His teaching, for He taught them as one having authority, and not as the scribes" (7:28–29). The scribes were accustomed to quoting rabbinical opinions as their source of authority. They treated truth as theory, often quoting many different possible interpretations of the law and rarely speaking definitively about anything. Ultimately, they substituted human opinion and human tradition for the authoritative truth of Scripture (Matthew 15:6).

Jesus came on the scene and, by contrast, He quoted no one's opinion. He said things like, "You have heard that it was said . . . But I say to you . . ." (Matthew 5:21–22, 27–28, 31–32, 33–34, 43–44). He spoke with divine authority. He had the truth of God. And He said so plainly: "I have many things to say and to judge concerning you, but He who sent

Me is true; and I speak to the world those things which I heard from Him" (John 8:26).

The wise spiritual leader stands on the very same authority. For us, it's not, "*I* say to you . . ."; it's, "Thus saith *the Lord.*" But it is the very same authority. And when you do that correctly and accurately, you lift up others and ennoble them.

That's what Paul did. He was not abrasive. He was not abusive. He was not arrogant or self-aggrandizing. But he was confident in the promise of God, and his words conveyed that confidence.

"I URGE YOU TO TAKE HEART"

In fact, far from being self-exalting, Paul's aim was to lift up others. The aim and the ultimate effect of Paul's I-told-you-so speech was to cheer and to gladden those men who were discouraged, disheartened, and in despair of their very lives. He promised them, with God's own authority, that there would be no loss of life among those on board.

Here is a fifth characteristic of every true leader: *A leader strengthens others.*

A real leader's aim is to make everyone around him better. He makes them stronger, more effective, and more motivated.

That is what Paul did here. He summed up his words of encouragement in Acts 27:25: "Therefore take heart, men, for I believe God that it will be just as it was told me." His confidence fed the strength of others. He built them up. He encouraged them to

> *Leadership Principle #5*
> **A LEADER STRENGTHENS OTHERS.**

believe there would be a future. He gave them a reason to hope when none of them had any hope whatsoever.

Then he gave them one more detail that at first glance does not appear so hopeful: "However, we must run aground on a certain island" (v. 26). Notice, he did not shrink from telling them the *whole* truth. This was not completely good news, especially for the owner of the ship. But it was still a better scenario than what everyone had come to expect in these circumstances.

Paul's complete honesty laid the groundwork for further establishing his credibility when these things came to pass. The men who heard his prediction knew this would either come true or not. If it did come true, they would know it was God who brought it to pass. What was the likelihood of landing on an island in conditions like these—losing the ship, losing the cargo—and yet not losing a single passenger? The sheer mathematical improbability was staggering. When it happened, they would know this was a purposeful display of God's power. Yet Paul was certain it *would* happen, because he had a clear and incontrovertible word from God. That was the basis of his authority. It would soon be the proof of his credibility.

Despite all appearances, God's hand of blessing was on this ship of disaster. Just as Paul's journey to the court of Nero was a blessing disguised as a trial, so this entire ordeal was a tremendous spiritual opportunity for these pagan soldiers and sailors. They were about to see the hand of divine Providence save them from certain disaster, and they would be given an opportunity and incentive to know and trust the one true Lord and Savior of heaven and earth. They would see His hand at work in a dramatic, vivid, and unforgettable way.

"I BELIEVE GOD"

Paul knew with absolute certainty what God was doing and what the outcome of their journey would be. He knew it because God's Word is infallible and His promises are sure: "All the promises of God in Him are Yes, and in Him Amen, to the glory of God" (2 Corinthians 1:20). Therefore Paul could say with absolute sincerity, confidence, and authority, "I believe God that it will be just as it was told me" (Acts 27:25).

In this we see a sixth principle of leadership: *A leader is optimistic and enthusiastic.*

Optimistic enthusiasm inspires followers. People will naturally follow a leader who arouses their hopes, and they will just as surely back away from someone who is perpetually pessimistic.

When I was playing football in college, the coach once made a speech I will never forget. We were visitors in some other school's stadium, and we were not playing well. The score was 0–0 at halftime. We went into the locker room and the coach began to give one of these Knute Rockne speeches. He got so enthusiastic, he put his fist through the blackboard. He began to remind us of our potential, punctuating his remarks by slamming locker doors and smashing boxes and laundry baskets. He made so much racket, I wondered what the people upstairs in the stadium thought was going on. His speech was a fierce, emotional, eloquent address about the superiority of our skills and the excellence of our team. He didn't berate us; just the opposite. His words were full of optimism and enthusiasm— and fiery passion.

> *Leadership Principle #6*
> **A LEADER IS OPTIMISTIC AND ENTHUSIASTIC.**

And his zeal was contagious. When the door opened, out we came, fired with new enthusiasm. I'll never forget it. I think we scored 48 points in the second half. People in the stands must have been thinking a completely different team came out that door the second time. In a way, that was true. We had caught our coach's enthusiasm, which in turn gave us a whole new enthusiasm. It was a great lesson to me about what optimism and enthusiasm can do.

I admit to being indomitably enthusiastic. At a Christmas concert in our church a few years ago, I was sitting across from a gentleman whose face was familiar, but whom I had never met. After the concert, I greeted him and asked, "How long have you been coming to our church?"

He replied, "I've been coming for more than a year."

I asked, "How long have you been a Christian?"

His answer surprised me. "I'm not a Christian," he said. "I'm Jewish."

I asked him why he had kept coming for so long.

Again his answer caught me off guard. He said, "Because I'm in sales, and I need to get pumped up. And you're so enthusiastic."

Obviously, that is not my calling. I'm not a cheerleader. But it is true that I tend to be enthusiastic. I believe what 2 Corinthians 2:14 says: "God . . . always leads us in triumph in Christ."

You cannot be an effective leader and be pessimistic. People who are cynical and gloomy debilitate everyone they speak to. They're like blood-sucking leeches. They make people pale, weak, and passive.

By the same token, you cannot be a good leader and bore people. I was at a Bible conference once with a preacher who seemed to think enthusiasm was unspiritual. Trouble was, his message was supposed to be about joy. I remember watching him go up to the platform with a sheaf of notes, which he carefully arranged on the lectern before him. He paused dramatically, looked up over his glasses at the audience, looked back down at his paper, and then read in a flat, emotionless, nasal monotone, "My dear friends, today I would like to speak to you on the joys of spiritual life." *Zzzzzzzzz.*

I don't think that's quite what the apostle Paul had in mind when he said, "Rejoice in the Lord always. Again I will say, rejoice!" (Philippians 4:4).

On the other hand, optimistic enthusiasm creates energy, excitement, and hope. We who know the truth of God and have the promises of God should of all people be optimistic and enthusiastic.

My realm of leadership, of course, is the church. I was recently reading a book on church leadership in which the author began with a dramatic pronouncement that if the church doesn't reinvent itself, adapt to postmodern culture, rethink its whole mission, and retool its methodology, the church will go out of existence in fifty years' time.

Of course, that is ridiculous. Christ said He would build His church and the gates of hell would not prevail against it (Matthew 16:18). Are we supposed to take seriously this man's warning that the church will go out of existence in fifty years if we don't reinvent our techniques?

I'm not at all pessimistic about the true church. I'm optimistic about it, because I know God's truth will triumph. I believe the church will be exactly what God intends it to be—glorious. Christ Himself "loved the church and gave Himself for her, that He might sanctify and cleanse her with the washing of water by the word, that He might present her to Himself a glorious church, not having spot or wrinkle or any such thing, but that she should be holy and without blemish" (Ephesians 5:25–27). That is going to happen. Christ's purpose for His church will not be thwarted.

If you look at the visible manifestation of the church in the world today, there might seem to be a lot of reasons to be discouraged. But if you look beyond that, understand God's purpose for the church, and lay hold of the promises, you can say as Paul did to those disheartened sailors on that ship, "Take heart, men, for I believe God that it will be just as it was told" (Acts 27:25).

That's part of leadership. Remember, the apostle Paul was on his way to Rome in chains. He might have been the *least* likely person on the ship to be optimistic. But as a true leader, he saw beyond the temporary circumstances and fixed his hope on the promise of triumph. And he drew courage and confidence from that. Such optimism was contagious.

GOD MAKES HIS SUN RISE ON THE EVIL *AND* THE GOOD

Something else gave Paul great hope and enthusiasm: He saw these circumstances as an opportunity to introduce unbelievers to his God. He wasn't the least bit timid about mentioning "the God to whom I belong and whom I serve" (Acts 27:23). God was the source of Paul's authority, his wisdom, his hope, his optimism, and his enthusiasm. Why would he be apprehensive about saying so?

Paul was eager to introduce God to these people. Under the circumstances, they might have thought they needed to prepare to meet Him.

Paul wanted them to know Him first as Savior, rather than as Judge. So he was bold.

He knew, of course, that the prophecy given to him by the angel would come to pass. And when it did, the glory and the credit went to God. As we noted earlier, the precise fulfillment of all Paul's predictions also established *Paul's* credibility. But it did much more than that. It put the focus where it rightfully belonged: it made these men see in a graphic way that God was sovereignly in control of their lives. They needed to glorify Him as God and be thankful.

Every one of those men owed their lives to the mercy and grace of God. They had made a foolish and reckless decision to sail from Fair Havens. But God was going to preserve their lives. And He was doing it for the sake of Paul. The angel told Paul in verse 24, "God has granted you all those who sail with you."

The unbelievers of this world don't know how fortunate they are to have believers around. Who knows how many people have been spared from judgment and disaster for the sake of godly people? A friend who happened to be on a flight I took a few years ago told me he felt especially safe on that plane with me, because he knew the Lord still had work for me to do.

That doesn't mean it's impossible for me to die in an accident someday, but there's a true sense in which that principle applies. Even the ungodly sometimes benefit from God's grace to His people. That was precisely the case with these men on Paul's ship. He was guaranteed ultimate safety because God wanted him in Rome. Everyone in the ship benefited from that.

The same principle runs continuously through the pages of Scripture. God's people in the midst of an ungodly community actually protect that community from disaster. God told Abraham He would have spared the entire cities of Sodom and Gomorrah for the sake of ten righteous people in their midst (Genesis 18:32). Later in Genesis, Laban begged Jacob not to return to his own country: "Please stay, if I have found favor in your eyes," he said, "for I have learned by experience that the LORD has blessed me for your sake" (30:27). The same principle is evident again in Joseph's experience. Genesis 39:5 says of Potiphar, "The LORD blessed the Egyptian's house for Joseph's sake; and the blessing of the LORD was on all that he had in the house and in the field." And even when Joseph was cast into prison, verse 23 says, "the keeper of the prison did not look into anything that was under Joseph's authority, because the LORD was with him; and whatever he did, the LORD made it prosper." So even the prison master was blessed because of Joseph.

And the men in Paul's ship were blessed because of him. Though they were lost at sea, without a clue where they were or where they might end up, they now had hope. They had a leader in whom they could be confident. They had someone who was not afraid to step up and take initiative. They had someone who had demonstrated good judgment, who could speak with authority, who knew how to strengthen others, and who gave them encouragement and enthusiasm. All Christians should be leaders like that.

As the story proceeds, we'll notice that the centurion, the sailors, and all the people on the ship begin to defer more and more to Paul's leadership. It was evident to all that the hand and the blessing of God were on him.

It is natural for God's people to want to follow someone like that. Pessimism, indifference, fear, and confusion melt away in the presence of such leadership.

Chapter Four

TAKING CHARGE

S
o Paul had some good news, and he had some bad news. The good
news was that not one life would be lost. The bad news was that
the ship would run aground on an island. As everyone on board
already sensed (Acts 27:20), they were headed for certain shipwreck.

They were in precisely the kind of crisis situation that calls for a
strong, clearheaded, courageous leader. And the one man best qualified
to fill that position and most prepared to step into it was the guy who
had the prisoner's cabin at the bottom of the ship's hold. The irony of
that must have occurred to the ship's captain, to Julius the Roman centurion, and to all others who were in positions of authority on board.
Paul had no official position, but he certainly wielded a greater authority
than any of them. He took his orders from God, and he spoke for God.
By now that was becoming clear to all.

True leadership is tested and proved in crises. The real leader is the
one who can handle the stress. He is the one who can solve the problems, bear the burdens, find the solutions, and win the victories when
everyone else is merely flustered, confounded, and perplexed.

That's what Paul had done. By now he had in effect taken charge. He
didn't usurp anyone else's authority; all of them more or less capitulated to

Paul because he was the only one with a clue what to do. And that is why although Paul began this journey as the prisoner (low man on the ship's organizational chart), all on board were now looking to Paul for leadership. The captain wasn't leading. The pilot was no longer even steering the ship. The centurion didn't take over in the chaos; he was evidently as perplexed and as frightened as everyone else. The only guy left with any sense of composure was Paul, and he was a rock.

This underscores the truth that leadership is not something automatically conferred by title or by rank. Again, leadership is *influence*. It is a matter of ability, not position. And as we read Luke's account of this shipwreck, it is quite an amazing picture to see all these powerful men, accustomed to giving orders and outranking others, suddenly looking to Paul, the prisoner, who had earned the right to lead.

NEARING MALTA AT MIDNIGHT

The ship continued to be driven by hurricane-force winds for days. The crew and passengers' panic was stretched out with intensity for days. The struggle to stay afloat was so intense that nobody ate for two full weeks. They were petrified with fear. They had not the faintest idea where they were. They didn't even know what direction they were going. The apostle Paul's assurance that they would all survive was the one last hope they had to cling to.

We pick up Luke's account of the struggle in Acts 27:27–29:

> When the fourteenth night had come, as we were driven up and down in the Adriatic Sea, about midnight the sailors sensed that they were drawing near some land. And they took soundings and found it to be twenty fathoms; and when they had gone a little farther, they took soundings again and found it to be fifteen fathoms. Then, fearing lest we should run aground on the rocks, they dropped four anchors from the stern, and prayed for day to come.

The Adriatic Sea, of course, is the narrow arm of the Mediterranean that lies between Italy and the Balkan Peninsula. In Paul's day, however, the Ionian Sea (the large, open expanse between the bottom of the Italian boot and Sicily on the west side and western Greece on the east) was also considered part of the Adriatic. Paul's ship was blown and tossed about in that vast region of the Mediterranean for two full weeks. That is a long time to be caught in such a desperate situation.

Then, around midnight on the fourteenth night, they sensed land. In the dark of a cloudy night, it would be next to impossible to see the outline of land on the horizon. That's why Luke didn't say they *saw* land; rather, they "sensed" it. This most likely means that they heard the faint sound of waves crashing on a nearby shore.

So they took soundings. That process involved lowering a rope with weights until it hit bottom. Then they would measure the rope and that would tell them the depth of the ocean. The first sounding measured the depth at 20 fathoms. A fathom is the length of two outstretched arms (standardized to exactly 6 feet). Twenty fathoms was about 120 feet deep. Deep enough for safety, but shallow enough to indicate that they were no longer out in the open sea.

They waited awhile and sounded again. This time they found bottom at 15 fathoms—90 feet. They were moving toward shore quickly. That was cause for panic; not an occasion for rejoicing. This was a highly dangerous situation to be in at midnight. They were literally washing ashore and unable to see what lay ahead of them. In water that shallow, there are frequently submerged rocks offshore, jutting outcrops that sink ships without warning. It was a sailor's worst nightmare. They were sailing blind, in the middle of the night, knowing only that every wave took them closer to danger. So they put out four anchors and prayed for morning to come.

They didn't know it yet, of course, but the island they were nearing was Malta (Acts 28:1). Malta is a small island directly south of Sicily. The geographical features of the region are in exact accord with the ocean depths Luke recorded. Experts who have studied maritime Rome also corroborate all the other details of Luke's account. For example, the distance from Clauda (where the ship last sighted land [27:16]), to Malta is 476.6 nautical miles. Let's assume this ship was drifting at the rate of 36 miles every 24 hours. (Nautical experts say that is about what we would expect with a Roman-style cargo ship in those currents at that time of year in a gale-force wind.) Drifting at that rate, it would take them exactly 13 days, 1 hour, and 21 minutes to be driven from Clauda to Malta. Add a day from Fair Havens to Clauda, and that's precisely two weeks. So it is, in fact, a 14-day journey from Fair Havens to Malta, if you happen to make it in a drifting ship being blown by a hurricane.

Judging from the data Luke gives about the depth of the water, they were less than three miles from the island. They could have been near the mouth of a large bay on the northwest side of the island. In modern times, that bay is known as St. Paul's Bay, though it may not have been the actual place where Paul came ashore. There is another bay at the eastern extremity of Malta, known as St. Thomas Bay, that some say fits the description more accurately.[1]

About the time they sounded for depth, they would have been drifting about a half mile offshore from the eastern end of the island. That is how they could hear the pounding surf.

Notice Luke said they dropped four anchors from the *stern*, which, of course, is the back end of the boat. That would automatically make the prow of the ship point inland. The plan, evidently, was that when daybreak came and they could see the shore, if it looked safe, they would raise the four anchors, drift straight in, and beach the ship. The winds were apparently still too powerful to risk sailing until they could find a safe harbor.

A THWARTED ESCAPE ATTEMPT IN THE DARK

In fact, the weather conditions were still so bad that some of the sailors tried secretly to abandon ship. Pretending to work on more anchors at the prow end of the ship, some of them had dropped the dinghy and were planning to use it to slip away from the damaged ship.

It isn't unusual for *passengers* to get nervous in adverse weather, but if you're ever on a ship and the *crew* panics, you're in real trouble. That's exactly what happened here.

Here is Luke's description: "As the sailors were seeking to escape from the ship, when they had let down the skiff into the sea, under pretense of putting out anchors from the prow, Paul said to the centurion and the soldiers, 'Unless these men stay in the ship, you cannot be saved'" (Acts 27:30–31).

At this point, Luke's record is filled with subtle ironies. First, notice that the men whom you would most expect to stay with the ship are trying to escape. Obviously, these men weren't the type of devoted sailors who stay at their posts even if it means going down with the ship. They were interested only in saving their own lives, even though that meant abandoning everyone else to certain death.

On the other hand, Paul, the prisoner, is the one trying to stop the escape.

In effect, Paul is now in charge of everyone. He's even commanding the Roman centurion. And the centurion and the soldiers are now taking his direction without question. Luke said when Paul warned them not to let the crew members escape, "the soldiers cut away the ropes of the skiff and let it fall off" (v. 32). That must have been a painful moment for Luke, who had "with difficulty" worked to help secure that very same skiff at the start of this ordeal (v. 16). The skiff was vitally important. It was normally the only way to get from ship to shore. It was quite literally their only lifeboat. But by now they had more confidence in Paul's leadership than any lifeboat. They immediately did what he said. They staked their survival not on a boat that could carry them to shore, but on a man in chains who could carry no one across the water. And once they cut the rope, there was no going back. From here on, Paul was their only hope. This epitomizes leadership at its supreme level, where people literally entrust their very lives to someone. It is a life-and-death risk that happens all the time in military combat, police work, and other dangerous duties.

Here's another amazing irony: Contrast verse 22 with verse 31. Verse 31 says that unless the sailors stayed in the ship, the centurion and soldiers could not be saved. But according to verse 22, Paul had earlier told everyone, "There will be no loss of life among you, but only of the ship." That promise, he said, he received from God by way of an angel. It was certain and definitive. There was no reason to doubt God's veracity, His power, or His sovereignty. God would bring to pass what He had promised.

And yet, Paul did not for one moment imagine that God's sovereignty nullified human responsibility. He clearly did not assume that if God has decreed the end, it simply doesn't matter what men do. He didn't think, *If God wants to save the passengers on this ship, He will save them without my efforts.*

Paul understood that God has not merely decreed the *end*; He decrees the *means* as well. And in the normal course of events, God uses ordinary means to accomplish His will. In this case, the means God chose for saving the passengers required the crew to stay on the ship. Without skilled hands when daybreak came, getting to the shore would be virtually impossible for the remaining passengers. God's sovereignty did not nullify the sailors' responsibility. In fact, God's decree is the very thing that established their responsibility.

Verse 22 of Acts 27 ("There will be no loss of life among you, but only of the ship") and verse 31 ("Unless these men stay in the ship, you cannot be saved") strike the perfect balance between divine sovereignty and human responsibility. There is absolutely no contradiction between these twin truths. Both are true. Not one soul on that ship was going to die. God had decreed it. Yet unless the crew stayed on the ship and brought it aground on the island of Malta, the passengers could not be saved. God had also decreed *that*. He ordains the means as well as the end, and that is why the truth of human responsibility is *established and affirmed* by the sovereignty of God. It is not nullified thereby.

So even though Paul was absolutely certain it was God's ultimate purpose to save every soul on board that ship, that knowledge did not prevent him from issuing a warning and directions to Julius, who needed to be diligent to make his rescue certain, by making sure the crew did not abandon ship.

In this is a seventh principle all wise leaders follow: *A leader never compromises the absolutes.*

When God has spoken, there can be no compromise. It's one thing to compromise on matters of preference. It's entirely different to compromise on matters of principle.

Compromise is good and necessary in most human relationships. In marriage, for example, couples often have to compromise to handle disagreements on matters of preference and opinion. In secular government, compromise is sometimes necessary to break executive and legislative logjams. In business, compromise is often a vital part of closing a deal. The person who refuses to compromise under any and every circumstance is obstinate,

> *Leadership Principle #7*
> **A LEADER NEVER COMPROMISES THE ABSOLUTES.**

unreasonable, and selfish. That sort of strong-willed inflexibility is sinful and has been the ruin of many relationships and organizations.

But when it comes to matters of *principle*—moral and ethical foundations, biblical absolutes, the axioms of God's Word, God's clear commands, and the truthfulness of God Himself—it is *never* right to compromise. The true leader understands that and knows where to hold the line.

In this case, Paul was not about to allow human ingenuity to raid the purposes of God. A lesser man might have said, "Okay, let them go. It's not worth the hassle." But Paul knew the promise of God was absolute. God would deliver every soul on board. But Paul would not stand by and watch these cowardly men vainly attempt to circumvent the plan and the promise of God. God was going to put Himself on display. He was going to show

Himself powerful and mighty. All would be saved from death, and God alone would get the glory and the credit for what He was about to do. But meanwhile, Paul would see to it that every attempt to thwart God's plan was itself thwarted. And therefore, in this instance, it was Paul's quick and decisive leadership that God used to put a stop to the crew's exodus and ultimately preserve so many lives.

Too many people are timid and fearful of confrontation in circumstances like these. Not the real leader. Real leaders have a clear understanding of what is absolute and what is negotiable, and they hold the line on the principles that truly matter.

For the *spiritual* leader, the absolutes are established by the Word of God. A leader who applies all the other principles of leadership can perhaps achieve a measure of pragmatic effectiveness. But *this* principle will test your true mettle as a leader. No one can be a truly effective spiritual leader unless he understands the essential truth of Scripture and refuses to compromise its absolute authority. This principle applies, I am convinced, not just to pastors and church leaders, but to Christians in any walk of life who desire to be good leaders.

DAYBREAK

Whether those renegade sailors realized it or not, Paul was doing them a great favor. To abandon a ship in the pitch black of midnight, in a hurricane, and try to make it to shore in a dinghy was foolhardy in the extreme. They certainly could not have known what was on the shore, or if there were rocks between them and the shoreline. They were simply in a panic, and they figured their chances of survival were better if they got in trouble in a small dinghy, as opposed to hitting the rocks in that huge, lumbering cargo ship.

Like all good leaders, Paul was alert. He also knew how to follow the chain of command. Rather than trying to handle the crew on his own, he got Julius to order the soldiers to take action. Their action, cutting the ropes and letting the dinghy fall off, assured that the sailors remained on board. It also meant that in the end, everyone would have to swim for shore.

Finally, dawn drew near. Luke wrote:

> As day was about to dawn, Paul implored them all to take food, saying, "Today is the fourteenth day you have waited and continued without food, and eaten nothing. Therefore I urge you to take nourishment, for this is for your survival, since not a hair will fall from the head of any of you." And when he had said these things, he took bread and gave thanks to God in the presence of them all; and when he had broken it he began to eat. (Acts 27:33–35)

These words identify an eighth principle of leadership: *A leader focuses on objectives, not obstacles.*

Luke had already mentioned in verse 21 the passengers' and crew's "long abstinence from food." Here we learn that for the entire two weeks of the storm, they continued battling the elements without eating any food. But now they had some hard work ahead of them, and they were going to need some strength. Paul, ever the clear-thinking leader, urged them to take some nourishment.

He looked right past the storm, beyond the urgency of the moment, and saw that they needed to prepare for the ordeal that lay ahead. While everyone else was still seeing the obstacles, Paul had his eyes fixed on the objective.

"This is for your survival," Paul told them, "since not a hair will fall from the head of any of you" (v. 34). You're going to be saved; you won't even be injured. But you need a good breakfast! (Again we see the perfect balance of divine sovereignty and human responsibility.)

Leadership Principle #8 A LEADER FOCUSES ON OBJECTIVES, NOT OBSTACLES.

Paul was getting them to forget their fears, the threat of death in the storm, the challenge of a nearly impossible swim to shore, and rather partake of the necessary nourishment they would need to make it.

I remember, as a football player, how I would come into the huddle in a critical moment in the game, facing a last-down effort to score, and say, "After we score, we're going for two! So line up quickly after the touchdown to catch them in the defensive switch." The strategy was to get people past the fear of the moment.

Paul did that, giving words of encouragement that ignored the very formidable obstacles.

Then, Luke said, Paul took bread, gave thanks to God in everyone's presence (thus reinforcing once again the source of his authority and his hope), and he himself began to eat. Here's a truth any godly mother knows: Two keys to serving the Lord are prayer and a good breakfast. Paul did not neglect the crew's physical needs and lecture them about the spiritual needs of their souls. He balanced the spiritual and the physical. Then he himself began to eat, becoming an example for all.

This is, in fact, a ninth important principle of leadership: *A leader empowers by example.*

Notice the effect: "Then they were all encouraged, and also took food themselves" (v. 36). Paul's courage became infectious. Everyone partook of the overdue refreshment, and it had the desired effect. They all began to feel better, stronger, and more hopeful. And then all hands set to work.

Here Luke records a crucial detail he had not yet given: "In all we were two hundred and seventy-six persons on the ship" (v. 37). Perhaps they did a head count during breakfast to verify the exact number of people on board. This would be essential later, when they regrouped onshore, to be sure that everyone had survived.

Then they set to work on one final task. The ship needed to be as light as possible when they ran it aground, "so when they had eaten enough, they lightened the ship and threw out the wheat into the sea" (v. 38). The remainder of the cargo, which had served as ballast until now, was dumped. Thus, for the owner and the crew of the ship, all hope of salvaging anything but their lives was gone. The prophecy was being fulfilled to the letter.

Daylight finally broke: "When it was day, they did not recognize the land; but they observed a bay with a beach, onto which they planned to run the ship if possible. And they let go the anchors and left them in the sea, meanwhile loosing the rudder ropes; and they hoisted the mainsail to the wind and made for shore" (vv. 39–40).

Here we see why it was essential for the crew to remain on board. Only experienced sailors would know how to do these things. The rudder had been tied down because of the storm. In heavy winds like that, the rudder would be impossible to hold for long, and the ship would have steered itself in circles. So it had been

> *Leadership Principle #9*
> A LEADER EMPOWERS BY EXAMPLE.

fastened with taut, heavy ropes to set as straight a course as possible in the storm. Now it needed to be free so the pilot could maneuver the ship right to the beach.

By the hand of God's sovereign providence, their course had brought them to a propitious spot—one of the few places in that vast expanse of the Mediterranean where they could try to beach such a massive grain ship. It wasn't a rocky cliff or a craggy shoreline, but "a bay with a beach."

They "let go the anchors," meaning, most likely, that they simply cut the ropes. There was no point in wrestling four heavy anchors aboard. It was clear to all by now that the ship would be a total loss, as Paul had predicted. They raised a sail (the actual Greek word used suggests that it may have been the foresail rather than the mainsail), and they steered for the beach.

They had no idea what was to come. They were headed for a virtual wall: "But striking a place where two seas met, they ran the ship aground; and the prow stuck fast and remained immovable, but the stern was being broken up by the violence of the waves" (v. 41).

St. Thomas, on the east side of Malta, perfectly fits the description of "a place where two seas met." Ocean currents converge there at the Munxar Reef, a submerged peninsula protruding a mile and a half into the sea. Breakers from the two currents come together right over the reef, causing waves to form in a unique crisscross fashion. Especially in a storm, the waves crashing together give the distinct impression of two seas colliding. Immediately under that place, the hidden reef is shallow enough to ground a ship.

From the ship's position coming into the bay, it would have appeared they had a clear path to shore, so they steered for it. But the ship ran aground on the shallow reef. "The prow stuck fast," and the violent breakers continued battering the back of the ship until it finally could tolerate no more stress and began to break up.

The ship was thus stranded some distance from shore. The raging winds and waves continued battering until pieces of the disintegrating ship were floating everywhere. It was clear all on board had no option but to swim to safety.

ALL HANDS SAFE AT LAST

At that point, the soldiers realized it was going to be every man for himself. They weren't about to go into those raging waters chained to prisoners. And in such a chaotic life-or-death situation, it would be virtually impossible to keep track of prisoners swimming free. But as we noted in chapter 1, if a Roman soldier lost a prisoner, he paid with his life. So they devised a plan to slaughter Paul and the rest of the prisoners to guarantee they wouldn't get away.

Luke wrote, "The soldiers' plan was to kill the prisoners, lest any of them should swim away and escape. But the centurion, wanting to save Paul, kept them from their purpose, and commanded that those who could swim should jump overboard first and get to land, and the rest, some on boards and some on parts of the ship. And so it was that they all escaped safely to land" (vv. 42–44).

Since Paul's wise leadership had not only endeared him to Julius, but also made him indispensable, the centurion halted his soldiers' plan to kill the prisoners. In different circumstances, he might well have authorized the slaughter. It was, after all, from the perspective of worldly wisdom, the prudent thing to do.

"But the centurion, *wanting* to save Paul . . ." Is it any wonder why? If there was one guy Julius did not want to lose, it was the man who had performed so admirably as a leader. So he ordered those who could swim to head for shore, and the rest grabbed boards, pieces of the disintegrating ship, floating debris—whatever they could find to keep them afloat, and they paddled for shore.

Imagine 276 people diving into waves powerful enough to destroy a huge cargo ship and every one of them making it safely to shore. The odds against it are astronomical. But that is exactly what happened. Two hundred seventy-six people jumped into the water, and two hundred seventy-six people met on the shore. In a maelstrom.

The first thought every one of them must have had was thankfulness to the God Paul worshiped. His promises are sure. His Word is true. God's angel had told Paul this would happen, and it came to pass exactly as he said.

Paul's triumph was the triumph of great leadership. Tested in the crucible of crisis, he stepped up and showed how a true leader acts. He was decisive. He was determined. He was clear thinking and levelheaded. He took control when things were otherwise out of control. And God honored his efforts with amazing success. He didn't compromise the absolutes, nor was he distracted from his objective by the obstacles. And he led by example.

In circumstances when lesser men would have been passive or given up, Paul took charge and became an example to all who are called to be leaders. It was one of the outstanding episodes in the life of this noble Christian, who by God's design has much to teach us all about the rigors and rewards of true leadership.

In the section that follows, we'll turn to some of Paul's own writings about the principles of godly leadership. There we find some wonderful insights into a true leader's heart, as the apostle battles a different kind of adversity—the disappointments and personal hardships a leader suffers when his own people stray from the example he has set.

PART 2

PAUL IN CORINTH: LEADERSHIP UNDER FIRE

Chapter Five
————

A LEADER'S DEVOTION
TO HIS PEOPLE

We move now from Luke's narrative about the apostle Paul to one of the most poignant, powerful, inspired epistles from the pen of the apostle himself. Here, and in the next few chapters, we're going to look at some key passages from 2 Corinthians. It is the most personal, biographical, and passionate of all Paul's canonical letters—and the richest insight into the quality of his leadership.

In the chronology of Paul's life, his relationship with Corinth preceded the Maltese shipwreck by about a decade. Paul first came to Corinth during his second missionary journey, in approximately AD 50. The shipwreck episode we have already examined occurred *after* his third and final missionary journey was complete, around AD 60 or 61. So as a prelude to our study of 2 Corinthians, we move back nine chapters in the book of Acts and one full decade in time.

Paul wrote 2 Corinthians specifically to defend his apostleship and to answer some major threats to his leadership in the church at Corinth. So he opened his heart very personally on the matter of leadership. In many ways this one epistle alone would stand as a wonderful manual for leaders. If we worked our way systematically through the entire epistle, we could fill a very large volume with insight on leadership drawn from 2 Corinthians. That, however, would make *this* book far too unwieldly.[1] So my goal in the next few chapters is simply to narrow in on some of the highlights of 2 Corinthians, glean the major principles it teaches for leaders, and try to sense the heart of a true leader by seeing how the apostle Paul bared his own soul to those who were under his pastoral and apostolic care.

To set the context for what we are about to study, we need to know something about the city of Corinth, the church Paul founded there, and the circumstances that provoked Paul to write this particular epistle to that church.

HOW PAUL BROUGHT THE GOSPEL TO CORINTH

Acts 18 describes how Paul first came to Corinth after his visit to the great city of Athens, where he had just given a defense of his teaching to the philosophers in the midst of the Areopagus, a court of the Athenian intelligentsia, named for the hill where it was located, next to the Parthenon (Acts 17:22–34). It was a forty-five-mile journey west along the coast of the Saronic Gulf from Athens to Corinth.

Corinth is located on a narrow isthmus that connects the mainland of Greece with the Peloponnes (the large peninsula that defines southern Greece). The isthmus is only four miles wide at its narrowest point, and that is where Corinth was strategically situated. Today there is a deep canal near Corinth that allows ships to pass. In the first century, however, ships were actually brought ashore, put on skids and rollers, and transported across the isthmus to the other side. All except the very largest ships traveling the trade routes between the Adriatic and the Aegean Seas usually chose this route, because the 250-mile voyage around the south of Greece was so treacherous and time-consuming.

From the most ancient times, Corinth was a busy trading center, boasting the best harbor in the Corinthian Gulf. But in 146 BC, the Roman army under Mummius destroyed the city and left it completely empty, selling all the surviving inhabitants into slavery. Corinth lay utterly desolate for a full century. A hundred years later, however, Julius Caesar rebuilt the city, populating it mainly with freed slaves. Thus Corinth in Paul's time was completely Roman in culture. It became a resort town, always crowded, always busy, and always filled with travelers. It developed a reputation for debauchery.

The chief attractions in Corinth were pagan temples served by prostitutes. The pagan religions of the Greek and Roman world had made fornication into a religious sacrament, and Corinth became the focal point for that kind of profane "worship." The entire city was filled with brothels. Row after row of them are still visible today in the ruins of Corinth. Ritual fornication had become so deeply ingrained in the Corinthian culture that in the first century, "to Corinthianize" was a synonym for sexual immorality, and "a Corinthian girl" was a euphemism for a prostitute. Everyone knew that Corinth was a city of unbridled vice. It was analogous to modern Las Vegas, except that its chief attractions were temples rather than casinos.

This was, perhaps, not an auspicious place to found a church. But Corinth also had a large community of Jews and an active and centrally located synagogue. There Paul found an open door for the gospel. "Where sin abounded, grace abounded much more" (Romans 5:20).

Acts 18 tells the story of how the church at Corinth was founded. When Paul came to Corinth, he met Priscilla and Aquila, who happened to be skilled in the same craft as the apostle Paul: tent making (Acts 18:2–3). Paul stayed in their home, worked alongside them during the week, and then, every Sabbath, he would go with them to the synagogue and preach the gospel (v. 4). They became devoted, lifelong friends of Paul, fellow Christians, and colaborers with him in his ministry (cf. Acts 18:18; Romans 16:3; 1 Corinthians 16:19; 2 Timothy 4:19). Silas and

Timothy soon joined Paul in the missionary work at Corinth (Acts 18:5).

A turning point in Corinth came when most of the Jews in the synagogue refused Paul's teaching. "He shook his garments and said to them, 'Your blood be upon your own heads; I am clean. From now on I will go to the Gentiles'" (Acts 18:6). He moved in with a Gentile named Justus (who happened to live immediately adjacent to the synagogue). Of course, Paul kept preaching the gospel, but now the focus of his ministry was the marketplace and the Gentile communities. Some Jews did respond, including "Crispus, the ruler of the synagogue, [who] believed on the Lord with all his household. And many of the [Gentile] Corinthians, hearing, believed and were baptized" (v. 8). That is why the majority in the Corinthian church were Gentiles from pagan backgrounds (cf. 1 Corinthians 12:2).

Corinth was one of the most fruitful mission fields the apostle Paul ever visited. As the church there was beginning to grow, Luke said, "the Lord spoke to Paul in the night by a vision, 'Do not be afraid, but speak, and do not keep silent; for I am with you, and no one will attack you to hurt you; for I have many people in this city'" (Acts 18:9–10). Paul's evangelistic ministry continued for a year and a half before he met any serious resistance.

Then, around July of the year 51, a man named Gallio became the new Roman proconsul of Achaia (the southern half of Greece). The Jewish community in Corinth tried to seize the opportunity to make trouble for Paul. They probably thought they could exploit Gallio's inexperience and convince him to imprison Paul or drive him from Corinth. "With one accord [they] rose up against Paul and brought him to the judgment seat [a place called the *bema* in the center of the Corinthian *agora*, or marketplace], saying, 'This fellow persuades men to worship God contrary to the law'" (vv. 12–13). Gallio wisely dismissed their charges, saying he had no desire to intervene in an intramural squabble over the nuances of the Jewish religion (vv. 14–15). "He drove them from the judgment seat" (v. 16). The chief consequence of the uprising was that Sosthenes (who evidently had succeeded Crispus as ruler of the synagogue when Crispus became a

Christian), received a beating before the *bema* at the hands of the local Greek community (v. 17). That may have been an indication of the remarkable acceptance and trust the apostle Paul had earned even among the pagans in Corinth. (Amazingly, sometime after this episode, even Sosthenes apparently embraced the gospel and became a fellow worker with Paul [1 Corinthians 1:1]).

Therefore, Luke says, Paul remained in Corinth "a good while" (Acts 18:18), pastoring the church he founded. Only in Ephesus did Paul serve more time as pastor. The Corinthian church was therefore uniquely Pauline, especially and personally indebted to the great apostle for his leadership. They knew him well and had every reason to trust him, revere his influence, and remain loyal to him and his teaching.

PROBLEMS IN THE CORINTHIAN CHURCH

Nonetheless, after Paul left Corinth, numerous and serious problems developed in the church there requiring skilled and strong leadership. When news of the problems reached Paul, he could not personally return to Corinth immediately, so he endeavored to lead them from a distance with a series of letters. We know that at least one letter from Paul to the Corinthians preceded the canonical first epistle, because Paul himself refers to that letter in 1 Corinthians 5:9, saying, "I wrote to you in my epistle not to keep company with sexually immoral people." That note of caution may have been the only significant point Paul addressed in that letter, because its contents are otherwise lost. He also seems to refer to another non-canonical epistle in 2 Corinthians 2:4, which he wrote "out of much affliction and anguish of heart." Those letters (although they certainly must have contained authoritative apostolic admonitions uniquely for the church at Corinth) were never meant to be part of Scripture for the church universal. The proof of that fact is that they were not preserved.

Paul's New Testament letters to the Corinthians are two comprehensive books about church life. Their implications for leadership are profound.

The first epistle makes it clear from the beginning that in Paul's absence, serious leadership problems had arisen in Corinth. The church was dividing into factions. People were saying, "I am of Paul," or "I am of Apollos," or "I am of Cephas," or "I am of Christ" (1 Corinthians 1:12). That spirit of division and conflict shredded the unity of the church, driven by envy, strife, and carnality (1 Corinthians 3:3). The problem did not stem from any failure in the leadership of Paul, Apollos, or Cephas (Peter). They were all godly men who labored as one for the same goals (v. 8) and all shared the same convictions (though they had differing leadership *styles*). The problem was carnality in the church, and Paul expressly said so (v. 4).

However, the division in the church reflected a serious leadership *vacuum* that had arisen in Corinth. After Paul's departure, Apollos had capably led that church for a season (Acts 18:27–28; 19:1). But Apollos had also moved on to other mission fields, and sometime after that is when the factions arose.

It is obvious from Paul's first epistle to the Corinthians that their internal strife and other troubles all stemmed from a lack of wise and godly leadership in the wake of Paul's and Apollos's departure. The Corinthian believers were tolerating immorality in their midst (1 Corinthians 5:1). Believers were suing fellow Christians in secular courts (6:1). People in the church were flirting with idolatry (10:14), disrupting the Lord's Table (11:17–22), and abusing their spiritual gifts. On top of that, someone in their midst was beginning to raise questions about Paul's apostolic authority (9:1–8).

That powerful first epistle seems to have resolved most of the urgent practical issues in the Corinthian church, but by the time Paul wrote 2 Corinthians, a new and even more troubling attack on the peace of the church at Corinth had arisen, suggesting that a lack of strong leadership continued to be a major problem there. False teachers, claiming a higher authority than that of the apostle Paul, had come to town and were systematically undermining the church's loyalty to their founder and Christ's apostle. They raised new questions about Paul's apostolic credentials and began to attack Paul's teaching and his reputation for their own selfish agenda (2 Corinthians 11:13). They were clearly taking advantage of the leadership vacuum in that church.

Piecing together the clues in 2 Corinthians, here is what apparently happened next: Paul seems to have heard about the threat of false teachers in Corinth, so he left Ephesus (where he was then ministering) and traveled to Corinth to try to help resolve the issues there. He had promised them in the earlier epistle that he would visit (1 Corinthians 4:19; 11:34; 16:5), so he seized this opportunity to go. But the visit, under the circumstances, turned out to be a deeply sorrowful experience for Paul (2 Corinthians 2:1).

Apparently, someone in the church, influenced by the false teaching, sinned against Paul in a public and humiliating way—probably by defying him or insulting him. Paul seemed to refer to this individual in 2 Corinthians 2:5–8 ("But if anyone has caused grief, he has not grieved me, but all of you to some extent" [v. 5]). In 2:4, and 7:9–12, Paul indicated that the episode prompted him to write a strongly worded rebuke in a letter (another non-canonical epistle), which he sent by way of Titus (8:6, 16; 12:18–21).

After that disastrous visit to Corinth, Paul originally had plans to go there personally twice more from Ephesus—once on his way to Macedonia, and once on his way home (1:15–16). But something made the first of his two planned follow-up visits impossible, and that is why Paul sent the letter of rebuke with Titus instead (2:1–3). He was actually relieved when this happened, because he felt it would spare the Corinthians some grief (1:23)—a letter being less awkward than a face-to-face rebuke. Moreover, Paul himself did not want another sorrowful visit to Corinth (2:1).

Apparently, however, he had already communicated his intention for the double visit to the Corinthians, and when he had to abandon the initial visit, his critics in Corinth seized on that as another reason to accuse him. They claimed he was vacillating and untrustworthy (1:19–23).

When some time had passed since Titus had delivered the letter, Paul was anxious to hear back from Corinth. So he began his third journey there ("This will be the third time I am coming to you" [13:1]). He stopped first in Troas, where he hoped to encounter Titus. "I had no rest in my spirit," he wrote in 2:13, "because I did not find Titus my brother; but taking my leave of them, I departed for Macedonia." There in Macedonia (probably at Philippi), he *did* meet up with Titus (7:6), who brought the good news that the Corinthians had responded to Paul's severe letter with hopeful signs of repentance: "He told us of your earnest desire, your mourning, your zeal for me, so that I rejoiced even more. For even if I made you sorry with my letter, I do not regret it; though I did regret it. For I perceive that the same epistle made you sorry, though only for a while. Now I rejoice, not that you were made sorry, but that your sorrow led to repentance" (7:7–9).

THE FAITHFULNESS OF A TRUE LEADER

It was in these circumstances, immediately after he heard the encouraging report from Titus, that Paul wrote 2 Corinthians. As we have noted already, the letter is the most intensely personal, passionate, and pastoral of all Paul's epistles. It is clear from the text that Paul knew there was still much work to be done in order to clear away the confusion the false teachers had sown in Corinth. He needed to defend his own apostleship, and he needed to deal with the leadership vacuum that had generated so many difficulties for the Corinthian fellowship.

Paul was loyal to the Corinthian church, and he wanted them to be loyal to him. Thus in the tone and substance of this great epistle, a tenth vital principle of leadership emerges: *A leader cultivates loyalty.*

This was no selfish longing for personal veneration (2 Corinthians 12:11). He wanted them to be loyal to the truth he had taught them (vv. 15–19). That is why, despite Paul's own intense dislike for boasting and self-defense, he vigorously sought to vindicate his apostleship against the lies of the false teachers. And therefore, as he modeled his own devotion to the Corinthians, he openly appealed for their loyalty to him as well. This is one of the central themes of 2 Corinthians.

Loyalty is a great virtue. We often forget that simple truth in the cynical age in which we live. Our society is so rife with corrupt leaders and so hostile to the concept of authoritative truth that loyalty is often perceived as a weakness rather than a merit. Rebellion and defiance have been canonized as virtues instead. "Who can find a faithful man?" (Proverbs 20:6).

But Scripture exalts loyalty. Loyalty is owed, first of all, to the Lord and to His

---

Leadership Principle #10
A LEADER CULTIVATES LOYALTY.

---

truth, but also to those who stand for the truth. Second Chronicles 16:9 says, "The eyes of the LORD run to and fro throughout the whole earth, to show Himself strong on behalf of those whose heart is loyal to Him."

Loyalty is a fragile thing. David prayed, "Give my son Solomon a loyal heart to keep Your commandments and Your testimonies and Your statutes" (1 Chronicles 29:19). Solomon himself urged all Israel, "Let your heart therefore be loyal to the LORD our God, to walk in His statutes and keep His commandments, as at this day" (1 Kings 8:61). But Solomon's own moral downfall came because "his heart was not loyal to the LORD his God, as was the heart of his father David" (1 Kings 11:4; 15:3).

Disloyalty is among the most repugnant of all evils. Judas sinned because he was a traitor. He had no loyalty to Christ, although he had been a privileged friend and close companion for years. No sin in all of Scripture is more despicable than Judas's traitorous act of treachery. Jesus Himself classed Judas's wickedness as more wretched than that of Pilate (John 19:11).

What do we mean by *loyalty*? Authentic loyalty is not blind devotion to a mere man. It is, first of all, an allegiance to truth and duty. But it involves devotion to the obligations of love and friendship as well. It is among the most godly and godlike of virtues, because God Himself is eternally faithful (2 Timothy 2:13; 1 Thessalonians 5:24; 2 Thessalonians 3:3).

Loyalty is essential to leadership. The wise leader cultivates loyalty by *being* loyal—loyal to the Lord, loyal to the truth, and loyal to the people he leads. Nothing is more destructive of leadership than the leader who compromises his own loyalty.

I have a very hard time hearing criticism of people who are under my leadership, because I am committed in my heart to being loyal to them. My instinct is to defend them. I always seek to give them the benefit of the doubt. My love for them includes an earnest desire to assume the best of them. After all, that is how love is expressed: "Love suffers long and is kind . . . is not provoked, thinks no evil; does not rejoice in iniquity, but rejoices in the truth; bears all things, believes all things, hopes all things, endures all things" (1 Corinthians 13:4–7).

You see that dynamic at work in Paul's dealings with the Corinthians. "I am jealous for you with godly jealousy," he wrote (2 Corinthians 11:2). And when he wrote to them with a severe rebuke, he said, "I did not do it for the sake of him who had done the wrong, nor for the sake of him who suffered wrong, but that our care for you in the sight of God might appear to you" (7:12).

Leadership is all about motivating people to follow. Therefore everything in leadership hinges on the leader's relationship to his people. It is possible to motivate people simply by sheer force, but that is not real leadership; it's dictatorship. And it never really achieves the goals of leadership. That can be accomplished only by a loving loyalty.

That's true in marriage (where loyalty and faithfulness are obviously so crucial); it's true for pastors; and it's true for leaders at every level. I have taught leadership seminars for the police department, the fire department, and to hundreds of the sales staff in the nation's largest auto dealership. At the core of the values I try to get them to see, so that they can lead people effectively, is the virtue of loyalty to those above, beside, and below them in the structure.

I tell graduates of The Master's College that they can be successful in any profession they choose if they do a few things consistently: Be on time, keep quiet and work hard, do what the boss tells you, have a positive attitude, and most important, be fiercely loyal to the people you work for and with.

Leadership hinges on trust, and trust is cultivated by loyalty. Where trust is born and respect is maintained, sacrificial, devoted service is rendered. Another way to say this is that our hearts have to be in our people, and our people have to be in our hearts.

Lord Nelson defeated Napoleon's navy at the Battle of Trafalgar, thwarting Napoleon's planned invasion of England. Nelson began that battle with the famous signal, "England expects that every man will do his duty." He could demand such devotion because he gave it. In fact, that victory cost Nelson his own life. He cultivated faithfulness and mutual loyalty in his men. A few years earlier, after a glorious victory at the Battle of the Nile, he had written to Lord Howe, "I had the happy fortune to command a band of brothers." That is the spirit of true leadership.

Paul was that kind of leader. His love for and loyalty to the Corinthians colors everything he wrote to them. Lots of pastors would have been tempted to give up on such a troublesome church. Not Paul. He was the epitome of a faithful leader.

CONSOLATION ABOUNDING IN CHRIST

Paul opened his second epistle to the Corinthians with an amazing expression of compassion and concern for them. He was writing at a time in his own ministry when he was suffering on many fronts. There was, of course, his intense grief over the problems in Corinth. Those issues weighed on him so much that he himself would testify, "I had no rest in my spirit" (2:13). On top of that, he constantly suffered almost unbearable hardship and persecution (11:23–33). Those sufferings were well-known to the Corinthians. But it is possible that the false apostles had used the very fact of Paul's afflictions to cast doubt on his authority, claiming Paul's hardships were proof that he was being chastened by God. So he set the record straight: God had comforted him in all his afflictions, and one major reason He had done so was to equip *him* to comfort *them* in their sorrows.

Paul wrote:

> Blessed be the God and Father of our Lord Jesus Christ, the Father of mercies and God of all comfort, who comforts us in all our tribulation, that we may be able to comfort those who are in any trouble, with the comfort with which we ourselves are comforted by God. For as the sufferings of Christ abound in us, so our consolation also abounds through Christ. Now if we are afflicted, it is for your consolation and salvation, which is effective for enduring the same sufferings which we also suffer. Or if we are comforted, it is for your consolation and salvation. And our hope for you is steadfast, because we know that as you are partakers of the sufferings, so also you will partake of the consolation. (1:3–7)

Here we observe yet another indispensable principle of leadership: *A leader has empathy for others.*

Empathy is the ability to identify with another person so much that you feel what he feels (cf. Hebrews 4:15). It is essential to true compassion, sensitivity, understanding, and comfort.

Paul was the one who had been wronged by the Corinthians. Problems in that body had *caused* some of his sufferings. And yet Paul knew the Corinthians were suffering too. Some of them were suffering, as Paul was, for righteousness' sake ("enduring the same sufferings which we also suffer" [2 Corinthians 1:6]). Others were feeling the pangs of repentance (7:8–10). Paul felt their pain, and he was eager to comfort them in all their grief. He assured them that his hope for them—his confidence in them—was steadfast. And his desire was for them to share in the consolation he enjoyed, just as they had experienced their share of suffering.

Paul had much for which to rebuke the Corinthians. And he did go on to reprimand them with some firm and necessary words at numerous key points in the long epistle. But it is significant that he *began* this epistle with such an expression of empathy for them. Despite their failings, he remained loyal to them and empathetic toward them.

Leaders must give their people room to fail. People need encouragement rather than scorn when they struggle. They respond to the one they serve when he has sincere empathy in their anguish and disappointment. People need to be built up when they fail, not further flattened. The wise leader doesn't ever

> *Leadership Principle #11*
> **A LEADER HAS EMPATHY FOR OTHERS.**

need to run roughshod over people. Leadership is ultimately *about* people, not just sterile objectives and strategies that can be written on paper.

That certainly does not rule out legitimate reproof and correction when needed (cf. 2 Timothy 3:16). But reproof and correction can be done—and should be done—in a context of empathy and edification, as Paul did here.

He was a faithful and compassionate leader, and his love for the Corinthians is therefore evident in every verse of the epistle. Such loyalty and empathy are essential for good leadership. Paul knew that, and as we shall observe in the chapters to come, it colored all his dealings with the troubled Corinthian church.

Chapter Six

PAUL DEFENDS
HIS SINCERITY

Dishonesty and artificiality are incompatible with true leadership. The leader who engages in double-dealing or deception will very quickly lose his following. Remember the first principle of leadership we observed in chapter 1 is that a leader must be trustworthy. Underhandedness, indecision, infidelity, and even ambiguity all sabotage trust and subvert leadership. And rightfully so. Insincerity is not a quality good people *should* tolerate in their leaders.

As we noted briefly in the previous chapter, false teachers in Corinth had seized on the apostle Paul's change of travel plans (he had canceled half of a planned double visit to Corinth), and they were evidently exploiting that incident in order to portray Paul as vacillating, unreliable, two-faced, cunning, and insincere (cf. 1 Corinthians 4:18–19). So Paul's first order of business in 2 Corinthians (after assuring the Corinthians of his personal devotion to them) was to answer that charge.

He does so in a thorough and tenderhearted way. First of all, he flatly denies the allegation that he had been insincere: "Our boasting is this: the testimony of our conscience that we conducted ourselves in the world in simplicity and godly sincerity" (2 Corinthians 1:12). He assures them that he has never spoken a word or written anything to them that was couched in deceit, concealed in double meanings, or otherwise deliberately misleading: "Not with fleshly wisdom but by the grace of God, and more abundantly toward you. For we are not writing any other things to you than what you read or understand" (vv. 12–13). And then he assures them of his wholehearted love and commitment toward them: "Now I trust you will understand, even to the end (as also you have understood us in part), that we are your boast as you also are ours, in the day of the Lord Jesus" (vv. 13–14).

He reassures them that when he originally planned his itinerary, it was his earnest intention and sincere desire to come twice to Corinth—once on his way to Macedonia, and again on his way home:

> In this confidence I intended to come to you before, that you might have a second benefit—to pass by way of you to Macedonia, to come again from Macedonia to you, and be helped by you on my way to Judea. Therefore, when I was planning this, did I do it lightly? Or the things I plan, do I plan according to the flesh, that with me there should be Yes, Yes, and No, No? But as God is faithful, our word to you was not Yes and No. For the Son of God, Jesus Christ, who was preached among you by us—by me, Silvanus, and Timothy—was not Yes and No, but in Him was Yes. (vv. 15–19)

Paul was saying that when he initially expressed his intention to visit Corinth (1 Corinthians 16:5; cf. 4:19; 11:34), there was no pretense whatsoever in his words. "As God is faithful," he said (thus in effect reinforcing his assurance with an oath), his communication with them was a well-meant "yes." He sincerely intended to come. And he *would* still come. But circumstances had changed the timing of the planned visit.

Then in what almost seems a digression, he reinforces the truth of

God's own faithfulness, and the utter truthfulness of the gospel message. Notice how he invokes all three persons of the Trinity to make this point: "The Son of God, Jesus Christ, who was preached among you by us—by me, Silvanus, and Timothy—was not Yes and No, but in Him was Yes. For all the promises of God in Him are Yes, and in Him Amen, to the glory of God through us. Now He who establishes us with you in Christ and has anointed us is God, who also has sealed us and given us the Spirit in our hearts as a guarantee" (1 Corinthians 1:19–22).

Paul was pointing out that his own sincerity as a messenger of the gospel was rooted in the truthfulness and trustworthiness of the gospel itself. And that in turn reflects the unshakable faithfulness of the Trinity.

Next, Paul explained *why* there had been a change in his plans. Once again he invokes a solemn oath to attest to his sincerity:

> Moreover I call God as witness against my soul, that *to spare you* I came no more to Corinth. Not that we have dominion over your faith, but are fellow workers for your joy; for by faith you stand.
>
> But I determined this within myself, that *I would not come again to you in sorrow.* For if I make you sorrowful, then who is he who makes me glad but the one who is made sorrowful by me? And I wrote this very thing to you, lest, when I came, I should have sorrow over those from whom I ought to have joy, having confidence in you all that my joy is the joy of you all. For out of much affliction and anguish of heart I wrote to you, with many tears, not that you should be grieved, but that you might know the love which I have so abundantly for you. (1:23–2:4, emphasis added)

In other words, whatever combination of circumstances may have contributed to the cancellation of Paul's visit, his own ultimate motive for postponing the visit was nothing other than his sincere compassion for the Corinthians. He did not want to come to them in sorrow (2:1).

He had delayed the visit in order to spare them the rod of discipline (1:23; cf. 1 Corinthians 4:2). He had not been insincere; he had acted merely out of love for them.

In this vital but often-overlooked passage of Scripture, we see highlighted three keys to Paul's sincerity. First, he always operated with a clear conscience. Second, he always sought to show himself reliable in words and action. And third, as the Corinthians themselves were well aware, his dealings with them were never self-serving or heavy-handed, but always driven by a genuine, tender affection for them. Here is why Paul's enemies were ultimately unsuccessful in portraying him as insincere or two-faced:

INTEGRITY THAT MAINTAINS
A CLEAR CONSCIENCE

Notice that the first witness Paul calls in defense of his sincerity is his own conscience. He had never deliberately misled the Corinthians, deceived them with verbal trickery, or even been purposely vague with them ("We do not write you anything you cannot read or understand" [1:13 NIV]). As far as his enemies' charge that he was inconsistent, Paul's conscience was completely clear.

This, too, is absolutely essential to good leadership: *A leader keeps a clear conscience.*

Remember, good leadership is a matter of character, and a righteous character depends on a healthy conscience. To see the role of conscience in leadership, we need to look closely at this amazing God-given faculty of the heart and mind.

The conscience is a built-in warning system that signals us when something we have done is wrong. The conscience is to our souls what pain sensors are to our bodies: it inflicts distress, in the form of guilt, whenever we violate what our hearts tell us is right.

The conscience bears witness to the reality that some knowledge of God's moral law is inscribed on every human heart from creation

(Romans 2:15). Both the Greek word for "conscience" (*suneidesis*) and the Latin root from which the English term is derived have to do with self-knowledge—specifically, a moral self-awareness. That capacity for moral reflection is an essential aspect of what Scripture means when it says we are made in the image of God. Our sensitivity to personal guilt is therefore a fundamental trait of our humanness that distinguishes us from animals. To try to suppress the conscience is in effect to diminish one's own humanity.

> ### *Leadership Principle #12*
> A LEADER KEEPS A CLEAR CONSCIENCE.

The conscience is by no means in-fallible. A defiled or poorly instructed conscience might accuse us when we're not really guilty or acquit us when we are, in fact, wrong. Paul said in 1 Corinthians 4:4, "I know of nothing against myself, yet I am not justified by this." He also acknowledged that some people's consciences are unnecessarily weak and too easily offended (1 Corinthians 8:7), so the conscience itself must be instructed by and conformed to the perfect standard of God's Word (Psalm 119:11, 34, 80).

Suppressing the conscience or deliberately violating it is deadly to our spiritual well-being. To disobey the conscience is itself a sin (Romans 14:14, 23; James 4:17), even if the conscience is ignorant or is misinformed. And to suppress the conscience is tantamount to searing it with a hot iron (1 Timothy 4:2), leaving it insensitive and thereby dangerously removing a vital defense against temptation (1 Corinthians 8:10).

Paul therefore placed a very high premium on the value of a clear conscience. His farewell speech to the elders at Ephesus began with these words: "Men and brethren, I have lived in all good conscience before God until this day" (Acts 23:1). He told Timothy, "I thank God, whom I serve with a pure conscience, as my forefathers did" (2 Timothy 1:3). In his defense before Felix, he said, "I myself always strive to have a conscience without offense toward God and men" (Acts 24:16). He characterized the positive benefit of the law of God this way: "The purpose of the commandment is love from a pure heart, from a good conscience, and from sincere faith" (1 Timothy 1:5).

A defiled conscience, if tolerated or suppressed, makes real integrity impossible. Until the wounded conscience is cleansed and restored, guilt will assault the mind. Repressing the guilt may ease the pangs of conscience, but it doesn't eliminate the fact of the guilt. Guilt and blamelessness are mutually exclusive. In other words, the person who dishonors and then ignores his own conscience is by definition not a person of integrity. A tarnished conscience therefore undermines the most basic requirement of all leadership.

Paul assured the Corinthians that his own conscience was completely clear. He had not lied to them. He had not misled them. He had not spoken out of both sides of his mouth. He could cite no higher authority than his own conscience to prove it, so he boldly did just that.

This was not any *selfish* kind of "boasting" (2 Corinthians 1:12). It was a candid and straightforward declaration from a sincere heart. Such a "boast" itself was proof of the very point Paul was trying to make: He had *always* shot straight with them. His words were always plain, honest, forthright, unflinching, and nonevasive—just like the apostle himself.

RELIABILITY THAT STEMS
FROM CLEAR CONVICTIONS

Next, Paul reminded them from their own experience with him that they had no grounds whatsoever to accuse him of ever being vacillating or unreliable. Not only had he always written and spoken to them in words that were clear and unambiguous (2 Corinthians 1:13), he had also consistently backed up his words with a life that was dependable and wholly in harmony with what he taught.

In fact, Paul said, the doctrine he taught was the whole basis for his constancy and steadfastness. Just as God is faithful to all His promises, Paul himself always strove to imitate that steadfastness by being decisive, distinct, definitive, and true to his word. Paul was the very epitome of a transparent man.

So again, he puts it to them bluntly and directly: "When I was planning this, did I do it lightly? Or the things I plan, do I plan according to the flesh, that with me there should be Yes, Yes, and No, No?" (v. 17). Had he ever said yes to them when he really meant no? In the question itself there is no hedging and no equivocation. *They* were the ones who needed to speak plainly: Were they in fact accusing him of double-dealing? Paul, in characteristically bold fashion, thus attacked the false teachers' innuendo head-on, and confronted the Corinthians with the absurdity of the charge.

Those who knew Paul personally certainly knew better. He had always preached Christ without equivocation (v. 19). "All the promises of God," which Paul had faithfully proclaimed, are themselves unambiguous and certain (v. 20). Paul himself had consistently been as definite and decisive as the substance of his message. So he once again affirmed that truth in bold language, with an oath: "As God is faithful, our word to you was not Yes and No" (v. 18).

Paul was eager to answer even the hint of any accusation that he had been double-minded or indecisive. He knew that such a weakness—even the mere suspicion of it—can seriously undermine people's confidence in a leader. Leadership cannot afford the luxury of drawn-out doubt and prolonged indecision. This is another in our long list of leadership essentials: *A leader is definite and decisive.*

Good leaders must be able to make decisions in a way that is clear-headed, proactive, and conclusive. They must also be able to communicate objectives in a way that is articulate, emphatic, and distinct. After all, a

> ### Leadership Principle #13
> ### A LEADER IS DEFINITE AND DECISIVE.

leader is someone who *leads.* Anyone can waffle. Anyone can be timid and ambivalent. The leader, by contrast, must give clear direction. People will not follow if they are not certain their leader is himself certain.

To summarize, then, Paul had always been definite and decisive in his dealings with the Corinthians. He proclaimed a message that was clear and unambiguous. He served a Lord who is true and faithful. And he had always taught them that all the divine promises are Yea and Amen. The Corinthians of all people knew these things well. With a little reflection, they would see that the false teachers' accusations against Paul were without any merit whatsoever.

TENDERNESS THAT IS EXPRESSED IN CLEAR COMMUNICATION

And yet, Paul *had* changed his mind and postponed the visit he originally planned to Corinth. So he explained why. He had made the change of plans for good reasons—not because he was being insincere or phony when he said he would come, but quite the opposite. His deep affection for them—which was by no means insincere—made him want to spare them the grief of a visit that would have been dominated by sorrow, rebukes, chastisement, controversy, and other negatives. Paul was by no means timid or afraid of such confrontation, but this time he chose to communicate his displeasure to the Corinthians, whom he loved as their spiritual father, via written correspondence, in measured and careful words—so that his next visit to Corinth might be a joyful occasion. *That* was what had ultimately made him change his plans.

Here is another essential principle of leadership, which I hasten to add as soon as possible after the previous one: *A leader knows when to change his mind.*

These twin principles go hand in hand. While leaders must be definitive and decisive, they must not be utterly inflexible. The best test of a leader's wisdom is not always the *first* decision he makes. Everyone makes bad decisions at times. A good leader will not perpetuate a bad decision.

Circumstances also change, and a good leader must know when to adapt to circumstances.

In Paul's case, his change of mind was forced by a change in circumstances. The irony of the false accusation against him is that Paul was not the one who was being vacillating and hesitant. The Corinthians themselves were, by giving undeserved credence to Paul's critics. Word

> **Leadership Principle #14**
> A LEADER KNOWS WHEN
> TO CHANGE HIS MIND.

had somehow reached him of what the false teachers were saying. He was both disturbed and disappointed to learn that the Corinthians—who owed their salvation to Paul's faithful ministry and clear, bold, uncompromising proclamation of the gospel—were being swayed by such far-fetched slander. The situation needed to be corrected. Rebukes, severe reprimands, and even chastisement were necessary. Paul did not want his next visit to Corinth to be characterized by such negative interaction.

Therefore he said, "*To spare you* I came no more to Corinth" (2 Corinthians 1:23, emphasis added). Though willing if necessary to take them on face-to-face, toe-to-toe, Paul did not want his personal interaction with them to be dominated by scolding and conflict. He wanted their reunion to be in an atmosphere of joy. He respected them and treasured the relationship he had with them. So rather than immediately coming to them "with a rod" (cf. 1 Corinthians 4:21), he decided to see if he could correct them by letter first.

And immediately we encounter another major principle all leaders need to bear in mind: *A leader does not abuse his authority.*

Paul had legitimate apostolic authority over the Corinthians. It was clear, God-given spiritual authority, confirmed by undeniable signs and wonders (2 Corinthians 12:11–12). But he used that authority in a pastoral, not an authoritarian, style. He might well have written to the Corinthians the same thing he said to the church at Thessalonica:

We were gentle among you, *just as a nursing mother cherishes her own children*. So, affectionately longing for you, we were well pleased to impart to you not only the gospel of God, but also our own lives, because you had become dear to us. For you remember, brethren, our labor and toil; for laboring night and day, that we might not be a burden to any of you, we preached to you the gospel of God. You are witnesses, and God also, how devoutly and justly and blamelessly we behaved ourselves among you who believe; as you know how we exhorted, and comforted, and charged every one of you, *as a father does his own children*. (1 Thessalonians 2:7–11, emphasis added)

He *did* say to the Corinthians: "I do not write these things to shame you, but as my beloved children I warn you. For though you might have ten thousand instructors in Christ, yet you do not have many fathers; for in Christ Jesus I have begotten you through the gospel" (1 Corinthians 4:14–15).

And here in 2 Corinthians 1, he wrote, "Not that we have dominion over your faith, but are fellow workers for your joy; for by faith you stand" (v. 24). He had no interest in lording it over the Corinthians. He refused to risk spoiling his relationship with them by repeated personal clashes. In the words of Augustine, "As severity is ready to punish the faults which it may discover, so charity is reluctant to discover the faults which it must punish."[1]

Remember that Jesus said leadership in His kingdom is different from worldly leadership for precisely this reason: "The kings of the Gentiles exercise lordship over them, and those who exercise authority over them are called 'benefactors.' But not so among you; on the contrary, he who is greatest among you, let him be as the younger, and he who governs as he who serves" (Luke 22:25–26). Paul was the epitome of a leader with a servant's heart. He perfectly fulfilled what the apostle Peter said every pastor should be: shepherds of "the flock of God which is among you, serving as overseers, not by compulsion but willingly, not for dishonest gain but eagerly; nor as being lords over those entrusted to you, but being examples to the flock" (1 Peter 5:2–3). Paul himself knew that "a servant of the Lord must not quarrel but be gentle to all, able to teach, patient, in humility correcting those who are in opposition, if God perhaps will grant them repentance, so that they may know the truth, and that they may come to their senses and escape the snare of the devil, having been taken captive by him to do his will" (2 Timothy 2:24–26).

Paul had set his admonitions down for the Corinthians in a clear and carefully worded letter, and he sent that instead of going to them in person. Until he received word that they had responded well to the written communication, he was not going to cast a pall over his relationship with them by another sorrowful personal visit.

It was a wise approach. It epitomized the very best traits of Paul's leadership style: loyalty,

> **Leadership Principle #15**
> **A LEADER DOES NOT ABUSE HIS AUTHORITY.**

empathy, compassion, tenderness, clear communication, and unvarnished honesty. That's why it was especially ironic that his enemies had seized on this incident to accuse him of *insincerity*, of all things.

Paul was torn. His personal hurt was real and intense. Perhaps the lowest point of Paul's life was when he wrote this epistle. He even said in 2 Corinthians 2:12–13 that when he went to Troas, he found an open door for the gospel, but he was so troubled in spirit over the Corinthians that he left Troas and went to Macedonia instead, in hopes of finding Titus and getting a good report about the church at Corinth from him.

In fact, the entire book of 2 Corinthians is colored by passion that arose from Paul's personal disappointment over the Corinthians' response to him. He had been severely wounded in the house of his friends. He had been devastated by the very people to whom he had most given of himself. Near the end of the epistle, he wrote, "I will very gladly spend and be spent for your souls; though *the more abundantly I love you, the less I am loved*" (12:15, emphasis added). He was over-whelmed by pain and depression over the disloyalty he experienced at the hands of people whom he loved and to whom he had given his life.

That is the price of leadership. It is a costly, lonely, and often thank-less calling. Jonathan Edwards ministered faithfully in Northampton for twenty-four years. He pastored his people through the remarkable revival of the Great Awakening (which Edwards's own preaching and writing had in no small way helped to ignite). Then his church dismissed him by an overwhelming vote, because he taught that only those who have made a credible profession of faith in Christ ought to partake of the Lord's Table.

At the end of his life, Charles Spurgeon, possibly the most effective Baptist preacher who ever lived, was censured by the Baptist Union in England because he opposed the encroachment of modernism in that organization.

But the leader must nonetheless remain gentle, compassionate, empa-thetic, and humble. If he becomes resentful, repressive, or ruthless in his treatment of his people, he will lose his effectiveness as a leader.

Who can do all that? Who has sufficient character to meet the high standard Scripture sets for leaders? In the chapter that follows, we will explore how Paul answered that question.

Chapter Seven

"WHO IS SUFFICIENT FOR THESE THINGS?"

I f you want to see proof of how important leadership is, don't miss the fact that Satan often aims his most ferocious attacks at key leaders. Among all the wicked devices the evil one employs, some of his very favorite weapons are half-truths and deliberate lies that breed rebellion and attempt to undermine the trust people have placed in godly leaders. Against the very best of leaders, Satan will invariably try to stir up a Korah (the rebel who organized a revolt against Moses) or an Absalom (the wayward son who led a rebellion against David's rule). That's why Scripture says "rebellion is as the sin of witchcraft" (1 Samuel 15:23). To defy a leader who is called by God and faithful to the truth is a peculiarly satanic sin.

It is therefore appropriate that Paul said the false teachers who had confused the church in Corinth were satanic emissaries—"ministers" of Satan (2 Corinthians 11:13–15). That is exactly what they were: tools of the devil, evil agents in his campaign against the cause of truth. They had deliberately focused their main offensive against Paul and his leadership. It was a strategic and well-placed assault, because if the powers of darkness could nullify

Paul's influence in Corinth, that already-troubled church would be completely at the mercy of the false apostles.

Paul was not eager to defend himself personally, but neither was he willing to abandon the Corinthian church to wolves. So he spent a considerable amount of time in 2 Corinthians doing something he found distasteful: defending his own character and credentials.

Paul's competency as a leader and an apostle was under direct attack. We've already seen how his *sincerity* was being questioned. The false teachers were also trying to provoke doubts about his *adequacy to lead.* They attacked his character, his influence, his calling, and his humility. They claimed Paul was not qualified to lead. He was inadequate, they said.

Paul masterfully answered that charge by turning it around against his critics. "Who is sufficient for these things?" he said (2 Corinthians 2:16).

In that very same context, Paul compared the ministry of the gospel to a triumphal procession. When a Roman general or a caesar won a key and decisive military victory, a formal "triumph" would be held to honor him and commemorate the victory. The triumph was a massive celebratory parade, one of the most important and colorful pageants in the Roman culture. The victorious leader would be carried through the streets with his army marching behind, holding the captured spoils and other tokens of victory aloft. Priests would accompany the parade, waving censers of powerful incense, diffusing a sweet-smelling aroma through the whole city.

When Titus Vespasian sacked Jerusalem in AD 70, he was given a triumph. Bas-relief figures on the Arch of Titus in Rome portray that event. Such celebrations were extremely rare, reserved only for the most critical victories. It was a once-in-a-lifetime occurrence.

But Paul said the ministry of the gospel is like a perpetual triumph. He likened himself to a censer through whom Christ "diffuses the fragrance of His knowledge in every place" (2:14).

Most Roman triumphs also featured a procession of chained captives. These would be enemy warriors who were condemned to die at the culmination of the procession. They would, of course, smell the aroma of the fragrant incense, but to them it signified defeat and death, not victory and life.

Paul said the gospel-incense ("the fragrance of Christ" [v. 15]) is precisely like that. It has a similar twofold meaning. To those who believe ("those who are being saved"), it is an aroma of life; but "among those who are perishing," it signifies death and condemnation (v. 15). So he wrote: "To the one we are the aroma of death leading to death, and to the other the aroma of life leading to life" (v. 16).

That is where he then raised the question: "And who is sufficient for these things?" Who is *adequate* to partake in Christ's triumphal parade and be an instrument through which the incense of the gospel message is diffused to all? Who in himself is qualified to receive accolades from almighty God for service rendered to Him on behalf of Jesus Christ?

He was turning the tables on the false teachers—calling into question their claim that *they* were adequate. He said, in fact, that they were guilty of "peddling the word of God" (v. 17). *They* were the insincere ones, making merchandise of the gospel. They were hucksters, con men, in it for money. They were willing to twist or shape their message deceitfully in order to maximize their profits. If it meant preying on people's fears, they would do that. If it meant trying to discredit an apostle like Paul, they would do that too. If it simply meant tickling people's ears by giving them whatever message they demanded, here were some ready teachers. They were the first-century equivalent of today's "market-driven" philosophies of church leadership and ministry.

Paul answered the rhetorical question of verse 16 ("Who is sufficient for these things?") in the first five verses of chapter 3. He said, in essence, that the only person who is really adequate to lead is the one whom God has made a leader. Self-made leaders are utterly incompetent. By contrast, Paul said, "Our sufficiency is from God" (3:5). That statement is the key to this brief passage and a summary of Paul's whole self-defense.

Paul was being attacked on several fronts: his character, his influence, his calling, and his humility. The false apostles who had successfully infil-trated the Corinthian church had relentlessly assaulted him by striking repeatedly at each of those targets. Notice how skillfully the apostle replied.

HIS CHARACTER

Paul was somewhat on the horns of a dilemma as he defended himself. He knew that no matter what he said in his self-defense, the false apostles would try to use it as proof that he was proud, egotistical, or boastful. They would try to twist whatever he said into another accusation against him. Yet he *had* to defend himself, because he was the founder and leader God had chosen, equipped, and appointed for the Corinthian church. If they wouldn't listen to him, they would not hear the truth at all. He was not about to abandon these people whom he loved to evil, false, spiritu-ally incompetent leaders.

Paul's response to his critics highlights another fundamental principle of leadership: *A leader doesn't abdicate his role in the face of opposition.*

The apostle had little interest in self-promotion; hence little interest in self-defense. He really hated having to speak in defense of his character. He preferred to be thought of as a low-level galley slave at the bottom of a ship, pulling an oar. He despised boasting about himself, rather than Christ. But he *had* to answer the assault or give up the church to false teachers.

No matter how unpalatable it was to Paul to engage in self-defense, he needed to oppose the threat of these bogus apostles for the sake of the Corinthians. They were in danger of being misled by the false accusations against him. If they turned against Paul and abandoned his leadership, they would be left completely exposed and susceptible to the false teach-ers' damning doctrinal heresies.

One truth every leader will eventually discover is that people are shockingly fickle. It's amazing how easily they can be swayed by lies about a leader whom they know and love. We see this all the time in contem-porary life. Sometimes it seems, the more a government leader tries to be a principled person of integrity, the more vilified he or she will be in the media. Gossip tabloids exist to publish deliberate lies about well-known people. Even the mainstream press seems bent on discrediting leaders who seem especially worthy of respect. The victims of such lies all know how fragile true loyalty can be. That's because

> ### Leadership Principle #16
> ### A LEADER DOESN'T ABDICATE HIS ROLE IN THE FACE OF OPPOSITION.

the fallen human heart is bent toward rebellion (cf. Deuteronomy 31:27; Acts 7:51).

That was true in Paul's day too. The false teachers had placed Paul in a position that seemed impossible. If he defended himself, that would only fuel even more charges against him. But if he ignored the threat, he would in effect be abdicating his leadership. Therefore, Paul wisely answered his accusers in a way that anticipated all their objections:

> Do we begin again to commend ourselves? Or do we need, as some others, epistles of commendation to you or letters of commendation from you? You are our epistle written in our hearts, known and read by all men; clearly you are an epistle of Christ, ministered by us, written not with ink but by the Spirit of the living God, not on tablets of stone but on tablets of flesh, that is, of the heart. And we have such trust through Christ toward God. Not that we are sufficient of ourselves to think of anything as being from ourselves, but our sufficiency is from God. (2 Corinthians 3:1–5)

Now, follow the line of his argument: He began with two questions directed at the hearts and consciences of the Corinthians. Did he really need to start at the very beginning and prove himself to them? Did he need letters of commendation to establish credibility with them? Both questions are worded in a way that anticipates a negative answer.

The "we" (used throughout the entire epistle) is an editorial "we."

It's not employed to be pompous, like a royal "we," but precisely the opposite. Paul used it as a humble substitute for the first-person singular pronoun. He was sensitive to the accusation that he was heavy-handed, self-commending, and self-exalting. So rather than giving ammunition to his critics who had made that charge, he appealed to the Corinthians themselves. Did he even *need* to justify his leadership with such self-commendation?

He would say similar things in 5:12 ("We do not commend ourselves again to you, but give you opportunity to boast on our behalf") and 10:18 ("Not he who commends himself is approved, but whom the Lord commends"). So this same line of argument runs through the entire epistle.

Clearly, Paul had no agenda to commend himself. That is not what he was trying to do. He was not setting himself forth as a perfect leader. In fact, in 1 Corinthians 15:9–10 he had said, "I am the least of the apostles, who am not worthy to be called an apostle, because I persecuted the church of God. But by the grace of God I am what I am." And here in 2 Corinthians, his only aim was to ask the Corinthians to search their own hearts and face for themselves the challenge that had been raised against him by the false leaders. Did they really need proof of Paul's character?

The false teachers had evidently insinuated that there was a hidden agenda in Paul's leadership—a dark side, a sinful motive, or a secret life others did not know about. They had attacked his character and were trying to destroy his credibility. So he replied, in effect: "You mean you don't know me well enough to know that is a lie?"

The frustration of Paul's heart comes through in the question he asks. All his labors, his teaching, his preaching, his prayers, his fellowship with the Corinthians and his ministry in their midst, his love for them, the tears he had shed for them—did all of that mean *nothing*? Did he need to go all the way back to the beginning and establish credibility with them all over?

Notice: he doesn't even appeal at this point to the miraculous element in his ministry, which had been clearly and repeatedly displayed in Corinth. Later, in 2 Corinthians 12:12, he mentioned "the signs of an apostle were accomplished among you with all perseverance, in signs and wonders and mighty deeds." But the *starting* point in his defense was an appeal to their knowledge of his *character.*

They knew him. They knew him well. They had observed his life. They had seen his godly character firsthand and up close. They knew what he was like from the inside out. To defend himself on that account would be utterly superfluous.

Thus Paul left the question with them. He did not boast of his own virtue. He had no need to do so.

HIS INFLUENCE

The second question is as disarming as the first: "Do we need, as some others, epistles of commendation to you or letters of commendation from you?" (2 Corinthians 3:1).

Letters of commendation are useful only when the person being introduced is unfamiliar. As we saw in chapter 2, Nehemiah needed letters of commendation to go to Jerusalem to rebuild the wall (Nehemiah 2:7). Those letters were essential to prove his legitimacy. They introduced him where he was previously unknown, and they showed that he had the king's support for his project.

Paul himself—in his life before becoming a Christian—had once sought letters of commendation for sinister purposes. According to Acts 9:1–2, Saul of Tarsus went to the high priest to get letters of commendation proving to the people in the synagogues of Damascus that he had authority to take Christians as prisoners back to Jerusalem.

Paul also *wrote* a commendation for Phoebe, a deaconess of the church at Cenchrea (Romans 16:1). Her letter of referral is a permanent part of the biblical record.

When the Corinthians sent an offering to meet the needs of the saints in Jerusalem, Paul said he expected a letter of commendation to come from Corinth with the courier who would deliver the gift to Jerusalem (1 Corinthians 16:3).

So letters of commendation are legitimate in their place. Modern job applications often include a request for written references. Churches require such letters for transfers of membership. To this day, letters of referral are a common part of everyday life.

Apparently, when the false teachers originally showed up in Corinth, they had letters of commendation. They most likely came to Corinth from Jerusalem. Acts 15:5 indicates that the *Judaizers* (false teachers who wanted to make circumcision a requirement for salvation) were a sect of Pharisees who had identified with the Jerusalem church. These men are called believers—no doubt they claimed to be Christians—but they had brought into the church the very same kind of legalism for which Jesus condemned the Pharisees (cf. Luke 11:46; Acts 15:10). Jerusalem was a hotbed for that kind of error, and many who taught it had gone out from the Jerusalem church to sow confusion in Gentile churches throughout the empire (Acts 15:24).

In all likelihood, that was the source of the trouble in Corinth. It appears, however, that the false teachers had come to Corinth with some pretty impressive credentials, including letters of recommendation, possibly purported to be from officials in the Jerusalem church. When they first arrived in Corinth, they had pulled out of their satchels these letters of reference. That was what Paul undoubtedly referred to in 2 Corinthians 3:1: "Do we need, *as some others*, epistles of commendation?" (emphasis added).

The false teachers had come into the church at Corinth as intruders, but they sought and found entrance because they evidently had impressive documents, addressed specifically to the church at Corinth ("to you" [v. 1]). They had come with an agenda, and they had planned well.

Notice that Paul also refers to "letters of commendation *from* you" (v. 1, emphasis added). Perhaps the false teachers had already sought and obtained references from the church at Corinth to give them further credibility when they took their error elsewhere. That was how such heretics plied their trade. They were always itinerant. They could not settle for long in one place, because their lives were corrupt. They were not truly regenerate. Sooner or later, the real character of their lives would manifest itself. So they stayed on the move. But they were in Corinth long enough to confuse and tear up the church—and long enough to get some letters of commendation from the Corinthians.

Paul was asking, "Am I in the same boat? Do I need written references either *for* you or *from* you?"

The thought was ludicrous. Paul's authenticity was evident not only from his own life, but also from his influence in the lives of the Corinthians.

You want a letter? he asks. *I'll give you a letter:* "You are our epistle written in our hearts, known and read by all men; clearly you are an epistle of Christ, ministered by us, written not with ink but by the Spirit of the living God, not on tablets of stone but on tablets of flesh, that is, of the heart" (vv. 2–3).

Paul's epistle of commendation was better than any letter the false teachers could pull out of their satchels. Paul's was a flesh-and-blood, living, walking testimony. His credentials as a leader were written in the lives of the Corinthians themselves. The influence of his ministry on their lives was ample proof of the legitimacy and the effectiveness of his leadership.

In 1 Corinthians 6:9–10, Paul had written, "Do you not know that the unrighteous will not inherit the kingdom of God? Do not be deceived. Neither fornicators, nor idolaters, nor adulterers, nor homosexuals, nor sodomites, nor thieves, nor covetous, nor drunkards, nor revilers, nor extortioners will inherit the kingdom of God." Then he added, "*Such were some of you. But you were washed, but you were sanctified, but you were justified* in the name of the Lord Jesus and by the Spirit of our God" (v. 11, emphasis added).

Remember, the effectiveness of leadership is measured in terms of influence. When you see someone's influence reflected so profoundly in the lives of other people, you have identified someone who is by definition a leader.

The only testimonial Paul needed outside the evident virtue of his own life was the fact that God had used his teaching and his leadership in such an instrumental way. God Himself had stepped into the vile Corinthian culture and carved out a church to His glory and His praise. The Corinthians themselves were an eloquent testimonial of Paul's influence. They were the living validation of his leadership.

By the way, this letter wasn't stuffed into a satchel. It wasn't folded up and hidden in a pocket. It was everywhere to be seen. It could be read by anyone, at any time, and in any language (2 Corinthians 3:2).

Paul also carried the letter with him, but not in his luggage. The Corinthians were written in his heart (v. 2). They were precious to him. "You are in our hearts, to die together and to live together" (7:3). If the false teachers had raised questions about his affection for them, Paul here dispelled that uncertainty with an explicit declaration.

Critics looking for a self-serving plea from Paul would find nothing here that could be denied. Christ, not Paul himself, had written Paul's letter of commendation in the lives of the Corinthians. It was a letter written without ink and pen from Christ by the Spirit of the living God (2 Corinthians 3:3). Could the false apostles produce a letter of recommendation signed by Christ? Certainly not.

Anyone can write a letter with ink. Only Christ can write a letter such as Paul had. The Corinthians themselves *were* his letter, kept in his heart, composed by Christ, and written down by the Holy Spirit. What purer proof of his authentic influence was there?

HIS CALLING

The false teachers had done all they could to undermine Paul's influence in Corinth. They had questioned his fitness to lead, and to some degree they had succeeded in getting the Corinthians to question his competency as well.

Paul, while vigorously defending his own adequacy, was eager to explain that his confidence was not merely *self*-confidence. So in 2 Corinthians 3:4, he explained the source of his certainty: "We have such trust through Christ toward God."

Paul was certain of his calling. That is *why* he refused to abdicate his leadership to the false teachers. His calling was a stewardship received from God. After all, "it is required in stewards that one be found faithful" (1 Corinthians 4:2), so Paul had no choice but to answer this attack on his authority.

Again, Paul was not defending himself for his own sake. He did not desire the Corinthians' affirmation for selfish reasons. And he certainly did not need to convince himself. But God was the One who called him to the role of leadership, and Paul never vacillated about his calling. This is another vital principle in all wise leadership: *A leader is sure of his calling.*

Those who are unsure of their own vocation cannot possibly be effective leaders. Nothing is more debilitating to leadership than self-doubt. People who have qualms about their own giftedness or calling never make good leaders, because at the most basic level they are uncertain about whether what they are doing is right. They will naturally be racked with indecision, hesitant, timid, and fainthearted in every choice they must make. As we have seen, those things are antithetical to the essential qualities of good leadership.

Paul never wavered in his confidence that God had called him to

> ### Leadership Principle #17
> ### A LEADER IS SURE OF HIS CALLING.

be an apostle. Others questioned him all the time. After all, he was not one of the Twelve. He was a relative latecomer to faith in Christ. He had, in fact, been a notorious persecutor of the church (Acts 9:13). Paul himself confessed that if his past life were the only consideration, he was "not worthy to be called an apostle" (1 Corinthians 15:9).

But the gracious call of God on his life, in spite of his past, was clear (Acts 9:15; 13:2). The other apostles affirmed him without reservation (Galatians 2:7–9). Therefore, while he considered himself "less than the least of all the saints" (Ephesians 3:8), he also knew that he was "not at all inferior to the most eminent apostles" (2 Corinthians 11:5; cf. 12:11).

This was not arrogance on his part; God had well and truly called him to such an office.

Such confidence is a great and necessary strength in leadership—to be so secure in your giftedness, so emphatic about your calling that no trial, however severe, could ever make you question your life's work. Effective leadership depends on that kind of resoluteness, courage, boldness, and determination.

People often ask me what I would do if I weren't in the ministry. I find the question impossible to answer, because I cannot conceive of doing anything else. I know beyond any shadow of doubt that I am called to preach the Word of God.

I have been told that I would make a fine lawyer, because I don't mind an argument. Several people have said I might be a good coach, because I like to motivate people. Others have told me I could have a fruitful career in sales, because I know how to be persuasive. Truthfully, I have never considered any of those things for a millisecond. There are no alternatives for me. Preaching is what God has called me to, and I simply cannot imagine myself doing anything else. I didn't choose a career because I thought it was the best of several options. I can completely understand what Paul meant when he said, "Necessity is laid upon me; yes, woe is me if I do not preach the gospel!" (1 Corinthians 9:16). Or, in the words of the psalmist, "I believed, therefore I spoke" (Psalm 116:10).

Those in secular positions of leadership likewise need to embrace their calling and be wholeheartedly devoted to the tasks they have been given. In the words of the Old Testament sage, "Whatever your hand finds to do, do it with your might" (Ecclesiastes 9:10). No leader can be truly successful who considers the present task a stepping-stone. You can't be distracted by the future and effective in the present.

The coach tells the team about to play a weaker opponent on the way to a critical game against a strong rival, "Don't look past this game or we'll lose." Teams still lose that way.

I've always believed that if a leader takes care of the present task with all his power, the future will open up for greater opportunities. Living in the fantasy of those future opportunities, however, debilitates us in the present.

Paul was a one-track person. There weren't any options or alternatives in his life. That is why he never doubted his calling or his giftedness.

People in leadership who indulge in self-doubt will always struggle, because every time things get difficult, they question the validity of what they do. *Should I be here? Should I go elsewhere? Should I get out completely?* Unless you have absolute confidence that you're called and gifted for what you are doing, every trial, every hardship will threaten to deter you from your objective.

I have never met an effective leader who wasn't competitive. Real leaders desperately want to win. Or, rather, they *expect* to win—to achieve the objective. That passion to attain the prize is what Paul himself described in Philippians 3:14, and notice that it stemmed from his *calling*: "I press toward the goal for the prize of the upward call of God in Christ Jesus." Paul knew that "the gifts and the calling of God are irrevocable" (Romans 11:29). He believed in the gifts God had given him. He trusted the power of God in his life. He knew beyond any doubt that God had set him apart for leadership, even from birth (Galatians 1:15). So he could set his eyes firmly on the prize.

Paul wasn't alone. All the apostles ministered with the same kind of confidence Paul had. Acts 4 describes how Peter and John were brought before the Sanhedrin (the ruling body of Judaism in Jerusalem) to give an account for their healing of a lame man at the temple gate. After they gave testimony, verse 13 says, "Now when they saw the boldness of Peter and John, and perceived that they were uneducated and untrained men, they marveled. And they realized that they had been with Jesus." The apostles' extraordinary confidence did not come from formal training. It came from the fact that Christ had chosen them, trained them, and empowered them with His Spirit. Even in the face of death, their confidence remained unshaken.

Therefore when the Sanhedrin instructed them, under pain of death, to stop speaking of Jesus, they simply replied, "We cannot but speak the things which we have seen and heard" (v. 20). Then they prayed, "Now, Lord, look on their threats, and grant to Your servants that with all boldness they may speak Your word" (v. 29).

That was the strength of all the leaders in the early church. Their confidence did not rest on their personal abilities. It wasn't *self*-confidence. Self-confidence is arrogance. But it was a strong and unwavering conviction that they were called.

Remember Paul's words, "Such confidence we have through Christ toward God" (2 Corinthians 3:4 NASB).

The false teachers came along with *self*-confidence. They claimed *they* were adequate. They weren't; they were peddlers of the Word of God (2 Corinthians 2:17)—corrupt, hucksters, insincere.

Who is fit for the task of influencing other men and women? Who is the authentic, qualified, acceptable leader? Is it the guy whose only credentials are written on a piece of paper? Or is it the one who has an untarnished reputation for integrity, the one who has a living letter of commendation written in the lives of the people he has influenced, and the one who has such a bold confidence in his own calling that he doesn't waver, no matter how severe the opposition?

To ask the question is to answer it.

HIS HUMILITY

Paul then made another statement that carries the same argument one step further and makes explicit what he had hinted at throughout his self-defense. Again, this is the theme and a fitting summary of his whole defense: "Not that we are sufficient of ourselves to think of anything as being from ourselves, but our sufficiency is from God" (2 Corinthians 3:5).

Although Paul was supremely confident of his calling and quite sure of his own giftedness, he also remembered where those gifts had come from, and he knew they were not from within himself. The source of his adequacy was God. Paul did not for a moment imagine that he was adequate for the apostolic office in and of himself. On the contrary, he knew he was inadequate on his own. About *that*, his critics were right.

"Without Me you can do nothing," Jesus said (John 15:5). The converse is equally true. "I can do all things through Christ who strengthens me," Paul wrote in Philippians 4:13. Both sides of that truth are equally important. "I labored more abundantly than they all," Paul wrote in 1 Corinthians 15:10, "*yet not I*, but the grace of God which was with me" (emphasis added); "By the grace of God I am what I am" (v. 10).

In no way did Paul imagine himself intrinsically adequate for the task to which God had called him. And that realization kept him dependent on divine grace in every aspect of his leadership. Thus he exemplifies another basic principle of all wise leadership: *A leader knows his own limitations*.

Those whom the world holds up as leaders often exude arrogance, cockiness, egotism, and conceit. Those things are not qualities of true leadership; they are actually hindrances to it. The leader who forgets his own weakness will inevitably fail.

Paul, by contrast, drew strength from remembering his own weaknesses, because those things made him more dependent

> *Leadership Principle #18*
> **A LEADER KNOWS HIS OWN LIMITATIONS.**

on the power of God. He wrote, "I take pleasure in infirmities, in reproaches, in needs, in persecutions, in distresses, for Christ's sake. For when I am weak, then I am strong" (2 Corinthians 12:10). When he came to the end of his human resources, that was when the power of God flowed through him. God, and God alone, was Paul's only true source of sufficiency.

People are not effective in leadership merely because they're naturally talented communicators, because they have creative minds, because they have a flair for persuading people, or because of any other natural talents. In fact, if your own abilities are all you depend on as a leader, your own limitations will be your downfall. From a spiritual perspective, human ingenuity and human cleverness tend to corrupt more than they help.

The apostle Paul had a great mind, but he didn't depend on it. He had wonderful training and he made use of it (or rather, God used it mightily). But he had no confidence whatsoever in the power of human wisdom when used for its own ends. He reminded the Corinthians that God's Word says, "I will destroy the wisdom of the wise, and bring to nothing the understanding of the prudent" (1 Corinthians 1:19). For that very reason, Paul's preaching in Corinth had been simple and plain:

> I, brethren, when I came to you, did not come with excellence of speech or of wisdom declaring to you the testimony of God. For I determined not to know anything among you except Jesus Christ and Him crucified. I was with you in weakness, in fear, and in much trembling. And my speech and my preaching were not with persuasive words of human wisdom, but in demonstration of the Spirit and of power, that your faith should not be in the wisdom of men but in the power of God. (1 Corinthians 2:1–5)

Paul had both the intellectual and the oratorical ability to hold his own with the greatest philosophers. And we see evidence of that in Acts 17, where he ministered in Athens among the philosophers. But that was not the basis of his ministry—either in Athens or in Corinth. The heart of his message was always Christ, proclaimed with clarity and directness, and he trusted the power of the gospel itself—not his own cleverness—to penetrate hearts and influence people. That's something many church leaders today would do well to remember.

The truth was not something that resided in Paul. The power for ministry did not lie in his abilities. Take the Word of God away from him and he had nothing to say. Remove the Spirit of God from his life and he could do nothing worthwhile. He knew that. His claim on apostleship was not in any sense tied to the fact that he was a clever speaker, a brilliant thinker, or a powerful writer. He was an apostle because God had called and empowered him. Take that away and he would not have been fit for the task, regardless of his natural abilities and his formal training.

That's why Paul refused to defend himself by boasting about his proficiency as a theologian or his skill as an orator. There's not a word in all his self-defense about his talents or his training. His only sufficiency was from God. Therefore, Paul could defend himself with the utmost humility.

Here's a principle to bear in mind: No competent leader is going to be anxious to impress people with his *credentials*. Leaders who are truly able are qualified because of their *character*. They are easily identified, not by letters of commendation, but because of the influence they have on others. They are people who are confident of their calling, and yet at the same time, they know they are utterly dependent on God as the source of their true power.

Chapter Eight

A LEADER MADE
OF CLAY

The false teachers in Corinth may have been personal acquaintances of the apostle Paul. At the very least, they had observed his ministry from a close vantage point. Somehow, they had become thoroughly familiar with his personality, his mannerisms, his looks, and his preaching style.

How do we know that? Their assault against Paul included the most savage kind of personal attack imaginable. They itemized all his personal defects. They denigrated him for his physical imperfections, his human weaknesses, the way he looked, and the way he spoke. In 2 Corinthians 10:10, Paul himself quoted some of the defamatory things the false teachers were saying about him: "His bodily presence is weak, and his speech contemptible."

Physically, it seems, the apostle Paul was not an imposing person. He was by all accounts unimpressive, perhaps even unbecoming. Paul himself knew he was anything but stunning in appearance. In fact, he made so much of his own physical unloveliness that some have even suggested he was a short hunchback with eyes so deformed that it was hard to look at him.

That may be reading too much into the biblical account of Paul's description of himself, but he did indicate in Galatians 4:14–15 that he suffered from a physical affliction that apparently had something to do with his eyes. He thanked the Galatians for not loathing or shunning him because of this physical malady: "My trial which was in my flesh you did not despise or reject, but you received me as an angel of God, even as Christ Jesus . . . For I bear you witness that, if possible, you would have plucked out your own eyes and given them to me." Whether he was describing a temporary sickness or a permanent deformity is not fully clear. But Paul indicated in verse 13 that this affliction was the providential reason he had first preached the gospel in Galatia, so I am inclined to think it was a temporary illness he had gone there to seek treatment for.

What is crystal-clear from the totality of Paul's writings, however, is that he often suffered hardships and ailments that were related to his own physical weakness. He was by no means a striking example of bodily splendor or a paragon of physical stamina.

The false apostles in Corinth had added Paul's physical defects to the long list of things they claimed made him unfit for leadership. Paul was unpopular, they said, because he lacked personal charisma. He was too homely. He did not have the physical stature, strength, and appealing persona necessary to command people. That, they claimed, was the very reason he wrote a letter to the Corinthians rather than visiting them personally.

They also impugned him as a preacher. They said his speech was "contemptible" (2 Corinthians 10:10). That may have been a comment on the sound and tenor of his voice, his rhetorical and oratorical skills, his style of delivery, the academic level of his content—or all of the above. Of course, Paul had already acknowledged that the preaching style he brought to Corinth was purposely devoid of artificial refinements and philosophical sophistication (1 Corinthians 2:1–2). But the false apostles portrayed that as something negative, so determined were they to diminish the Corinthians' estimation of their spiritual father. They claimed Paul's appearance and style were so poor and blemished that he had become a detriment to the gospel message.

It was probably true that Paul didn't try to impress anyone with his cleverness, his intellect, or his looks. Whatever lies the false apostles had spread about Paul, on this point they were surely right: Nothing about his style or appearance contributed any power to his message. So they tried to turn that into an excuse to mock and scorn him.

It was an ugly, impertinent, hurtful, embarrassing, and unduly personal attack on a noble man. On a purely private level, he no doubt would have preferred to ignore it and suffer such abuse for Christ's sake (cf. 1 Peter 2:20–23). But once again, out of concern for the Corinthians, he had no choice but to respond. For the truth's sake, he needed to defend his apostleship by exposing and opposing the false apostles' deceit. Otherwise, the Corinthians would be devoured by their false teaching.

How would Paul handle *this* attack without seeming self-aggrandizing or narcissistic? He certainly could not claim that they were wrong and he was really quite appealing. He couldn't write back and say, "Look, I just found three people who think I'm cute." His physical infirmities were not news to him. In fact, no one knew his own weakness better than the apostle Paul. But, frankly, he was being criticized by people who were much more sinful and weak than he was. How could he defend himself against such intensely personal vilification without appearing proud?

He answered this attack exactly as he had already answered the false apostles' other criticisms: by honestly and humbly acknowledging his own inherent insufficiency. The gist of his reply is summed up in 2 Corinthians 12:9: "most gladly I will rather boast in my infirmities."

It was, quite frankly, a matter of constant amazement to Paul himself that he was ever called to leadership to begin with. He told Timothy, "I thank Christ Jesus our Lord who has enabled me, because He counted me faithful, putting me into the ministry, although I was formerly a blasphemer, a persecutor, and an insolent man" (1 Timothy 1:12–13). If the truth were told, he had to agree with his accusers' claims. In effect, he acknowledged that they were exactly right on this count. Everything they said about his human weaknesses was true. He wasn't attractive. He wasn't anything special.

But after all, he reminded the Corinthians, "we do not preach ourselves, but Christ Jesus the Lord, and ourselves your bondservants for Jesus' sake" (2 Corinthians 4:5).

In other words, it wasn't about *Paul* in the first place. He was only a bondservant and a messenger whose role was to proclaim the grandeur, the majesty, and the wonder of the new covenant message—"the knowledge of the glory of God in the face of Jesus Christ" (v. 6).

Paul freely admitted that in his case, the message was packaged in a humble, frail, imperfect, common container. Remember the imagery he employed in 2 Corinthians 2. He was a censer—a vessel to hold the gospel incense. He was merely an instrument through which God "diffuses the fragrance of His knowledge in every place" (2:14).

And what a humble vessel he was! Not a fancy, engraved censer made of precious metals and inlaid with fine jewels, but an average, everyday clay pot.

That is precisely what he said in 4:7: "We have this treasure in earthen vessels, that the excellence of the power may be of God and not of us." An earthenware jar. A terra-cotta container.

The imagery is drawn from a familiar Old Testament passage in Jeremiah 18, where God is portrayed as a sovereign Potter, making and remaking His creatures into vessels fit for whatever use He chooses. Jeremiah wrote:

> I went down to the potter's house, and there he was, making something at the wheel. And the vessel that he made of clay was marred in the hand of the potter; so he made it again into another vessel, as it seemed good to the potter to make. Then the

word of the LORD came to me, saying: "O house of Israel, can I
not do with you as this potter?" says the LORD. "Look, as the clay
is in the potter's hand, so are you in My hand, O house of Israel!"
(18:3–6)

Paul borrowed the same familiar imagery in Romans 9:21: "Does not
the potter have power over the clay, from the same lump to make one vessel for honor and another for dishonor?" The clay represents fallen
humanity—base, dirty, messy, and without any inherent virtue or excellence of its own. As the divine Potter, God sovereignly molds different
vessels "from the same lump" for whatever use He sees fit. Their usefulness is derived from the work of the Potter, certainly not owing to any
quality in the clay.

Even the finished clay pots have no virtue or power of their own. They
are simply instruments in the Potter's hands, fashioned by Him according
to His own good pleasure. Isaiah wrote, "Woe to the one who quarrels
with his Maker—an earthenware vessel among the vessels of earth! Will
the clay say to the potter, 'What are you doing?'" (Isaiah 45:9 NASB).

So Paul didn't deny his status as a lowly jar of clay; he admitted it.
That was no reason to reject him, though. In fact, his lowly estate as a clay
vessel was one of the credentials of his apostleship. Thus he once again
turned the tables on his accusers.

All leaders are at best clay pots. Some may be better-looking pots than
others. But no true leader can boast of having attained his position merely
because of superior talents, physical attributes, communication skills, or
whatever. If God did not use homely, ordinary clay pots, there wouldn't
be any spiritual leaders at all, because there aren't any people who aren't
beset with blemishes and human weaknesses.

The greatest of all leaders in Scripture were fundamentally flawed.
Abraham gave in to his fears and shamefully lied (Genesis 12:13; 20:2).
Moses freely acknowledged that he was "slow of speech and slow of

tongue" (Exodus 4:10). He also had repeated problems with a fiery temper (Exodus 2:11–12; Numbers 20:11–12). David committed adultery and murder (2 Samuel 11). Elijah succumbed to fear and depression (1 Kings 19:3–10). Isaiah confessed that he had a dirty mouth (Isaiah 6:5). Jonah tried to flee his prophetic commission because he hated the people to whom God called him to minister (Jonah 4:1–3). Most of the Twelve whom Christ appointed were crude fishermen. On the night of Christ's betrayal, they all "forsook Him and fled" (Matthew 26:56). Peter, their leader and spokesman, had repeatedly embarrassed himself by saying and doing impetuous things. Then on that terrible night, he verbally denied Christ with cursing and oaths (Matthew 26:69–74). Peter himself confessed that he was a sinful man (Luke 5:8). The apostle John and his brother, James, in the spirit of Jonah, wanted to call down fire from heaven to destroy people whom Christ had come to save (Luke 9:54–56). James and John (in a blatant display of sinful pride) also conspired with their mother to ask Jesus to grant them thrones in the kingdom on Christ's right and left hands (Matthew 20:20–24). All of these were fragile, imperfect men of clay.

Like every such earthenware vessel, Paul had imperfections too. He graphically described his own struggle with indwelling sin—especially the sin of evil desire (Romans 7:8–23). He even referred to himself as a "wretched man" (v. 24).

But the weaknesses he was being attacked for in Corinth were not any sinful tendencies. They were normal human limitations—physical frailties, supposed shortcomings in his leadership style, alleged defects in the way he communicated, underachievements, and whatnot. Paul had no need to deny such accusations. Rather, he embraced his own weaknesses and showed how those very weaknesses were further credentials of his legitimacy as a leader.

Notice that he saw no need to defend his apostleship by citing his own past achievements, by defending his natural talents, or by otherwise promoting himself in the eyes of the Corinthians. Instead, he explained how the very same qualities that made him a lowly clay pot also equipped him to lead.

CLAY POTS ARE HUMBLE

There's a deliberate paradox in 2 Corinthians 4:7: "treasure in earthen vessels." Treasure is normally stored in more elaborate containers than earthenware, of course. Jewels are set in gold. Gold is often displayed in ivory or alabaster containers, decorated with fine handiwork. Few would think a plain terra-cotta pot is a suitable container for something inherently invaluable. It's too modest, too ordinary, too humble.

"But," Paul wrote, "we have this treasure in earthen vessels." The "treasure" he spoke of is the promise of the new covenant (2 Corinthians 3:7–18), the gospel message (4:3), "the light of the knowledge of the glory of God in the face of Jesus Christ" (4:6).

Why is such a priceless treasure contained in clay pots? "[So] that the excellence of the power may be of God and not of us" (v. 7). The more feeble the vessel, the more evident it is that the power is God's.

Paul was not about to get into a debate with the false apostles over whose looks or oratorical ability were superior. He said in 10:12, "We dare not class ourselves or compare ourselves with those who commend themselves. But they, measuring themselves by themselves, and comparing themselves among themselves, are not wise." He wasn't the least bit interested in weighing himself against men who measured themselves by such superficial standards. "But," he said (paraphrasing Jeremiah 9:23) "'he who glories, let him glory in the LORD.' For not he who commends himself is approved, but whom the Lord commends" (2 Corinthians 10:17–18).

The Lord *had* commended Paul, notwithstanding what he looked like or talked like. Paul was quite content to be a clay pot in the service of the Lord. He was seeking not the approval of men but the eternal "well done" of the heavenly Judge.

Consider again the nature of a clay pot. It is simply baked clay. Dirt baked hard. God knows that is what we all are—though we have a tendency to forget. "He knows our frame; He remembers that we are dust" (Psalm 103:14). He said to Adam, "Dust you are, and to dust you shall return" (Genesis 3:19).

Paul said, in effect, "That's all I am: kiln-dried mud."

Clay pots were a common feature in Paul's day. They served many functions. Every kind of household vessel was made of clay, from tableware to washbasins and garbage containers. Baked clay was cheap, breakable, replaceable, and unattractive.

In 2 Timothy 2:20, Paul wrote, "In a great house there are not only vessels of gold and silver, but also of wood and clay, some for honor and some for dishonor." Honorable vessels would include fine tableware, decorative earthenware, goblets, water pots, pitchers, and other utensils reserved for meals and formal occasions. Dishonorable vessels would include chamber pots, garbage receptacles, and other items for unclean uses. Most of the dishonorable vessels were made of clay. None of them had any intrinsic value.

Occasionally, clay pots were used as simple, inexpensive vaults, especially when a treasure was meant to be hidden. Priceless jewelry, gold, silver, title deeds, valuable documents, or other treasured items could be sealed in a clay jar and buried in the ground to keep them safe and hidden. That is how the man plowing a field in the famous parable of Matthew 13:44 might have uncovered hidden treasure. His plow might have broken a clay container and thereby unearthed the treasure. In fact, that is precisely how the Dead Sea Scrolls were discovered in the caves at Qumran. A shepherd boy, working in those hills, threw a rock into a cave and heard a clay jar break. Inside were priceless manuscripts.

But Paul was describing a treasure meant to be put on display, not hidden. His emphasis was on the trivial importance of the container, compared to the priceless value of what it held. He was admitting that his critics might well denigrate his looks, vilify his manner of speech, or point to his other weaknesses. He wouldn't even try to defend himself on those grounds. What did they expect from a garbage pail? Paul said he was the chief of sinners (1 Timothy 1:15). As far as he was concerned, his own merits were worthless. He counted them as dung, excrement, the lowest kind of filth (Philippians 3:8). If it weren't for the priceless treasure God had entrusted to him, he would have no value at all.

That is true humility, and it is one of the keys to Paul's effectiveness as a leader. Since the day of his conversion on the road to Damascus, he had never thought of himself as anyone special. Quite the contrary. As we saw in the previous chapter, he regarded himself as "least of the apostles" (1 Corinthians 15:9); "less than the least of all the saints" (Ephesians 3:8); "formerly a blasphemer, a persecutor, and an insolent man" (1 Timothy 1:13); a "wretched man" (Romans 7:24).

But God delights in choosing menial, plain, foolish, common, despised, ignoble people, whom society might say are good for nothing. The Corinthians themselves knew this full well. Some of them had been fornicators, idolaters, thieves, drunkards, and worse (1 Corinthians 6:9–11). Paul could easily point to them as proof that God calls base and lowly people. In fact, Paul already had done so:

> You see your calling, brethren, that not many wise according to the flesh, not many mighty, not many noble, are called. But God has chosen the foolish things of the world to put to shame the wise, and God has chosen the weak things of the world to put to shame the things which are mighty; and the base things of the world and the things which are despised God has chosen, and the things which are not, to bring to nothing the things that are, that no flesh should glory in His presence. (1 Corinthians 1:26–29)

By using common, ordinary clay pots, God puts His glory on display in bold relief. The Corinthians of all people knew that was true.

I occasionally hear Christians say, "Wouldn't it be wonderful if that famous person over there, or this stunning beauty over here, or some great genius in the academic world became a Christian? Wouldn't they be amazing spokespeople for Christ? What an impact they could have!" God does occasionally use such people, but as Paul says, "not many." He generally ignores that strategy and employs plain clay pots—in order that it may be clear to all that the power is of God and not from us. Even the notable and talented of this world must learn to become clay pots in order to be used by God to maximum effectiveness.

In Christ's day the world was filled with intellectuals and influential people. There were celebrated philosophers in Athens, unsurpassed scholars in Alexandria, the most powerful political leaders the world had ever known in Rome, and some of the most meticulous rabbis of all time in and around Jerusalem. Christ bypassed them all and called simple, crude, unknown, and uneducated fishermen from Galilee to be His disciples.

So Paul said, "You know what? You're right. *By myself,* I'm good for nothing but taking out the garbage." In the words of Romans 7:18, "I know that in me (that is, in my flesh) nothing good dwells." But *by God's grace,* he was an ugly jar that contained an immense treasure.

God's own power was made manifest in Paul because he did not get in the way. That's why he said, "Most gladly I will rather boast in my infirmities, that the power of Christ may rest upon me. Therefore I take pleasure in infirmities, in reproaches, in needs, in persecutions, in distresses, for Christ's sake. For when I am weak, then I am strong" (2 Corinthians 12:9–10).

God is still bypassing the elite. He's leaving the proud intellectuals in universities and seminaries, and He's looking for clay pots who will carry the treasure of saving truth with humility. By using frail and common people, God makes it clear that the power is His, not ours. The fact that God can make spiritual leaders out of such unsightly clay jars is proof of the greatness of His power. Spiritual power is not the product of human genius or human technique. The power is from God.

And the wonderful thing is that our weakness doesn't prove fatal to the cause of truth. In fact, it is advantageous, because it gets us out of the way and lets the power of God do its work. The great and encouraging reality of our calling as spiritual leaders is this: Knowing our weakness isn't a disadvantage; it is essential to what we do as leaders. And therefore, with Paul, we can rejoice in that weakness.

It is important to remember that we are not talking about sin; we are talking about normal human limitations. Because of the weakness of our flesh, we *do* sin (1 John 1:8)—but sin itself is never to be tolerated or gloried in. Sin—especially willful sin or unrepentant sin—is seriously detrimental to leadership. As we shall see in chapter 10, sin can even permanently disqualify a person from spiritual leadership.

The humility that stems from knowing our human frailties ought to motivate us to hate sin and to be constantly and continuously repentant. That was the spirit of the apostle Paul himself, as we see in Romans 7. Every true spiritual leader will cultivate a holy hatred for sin and a humble, repentant heart over sin in his own life. That is an essential part of the life of every humble clay pot.

CLAY POTS ARE STURDY

Although clay pots are cheap, ordinary, and disposable, they are also amazingly durable. They can survive enormous amounts of stress and rough handling. Even if chipped, they can still be useful. You can scour them all you want and they simply won't wear out. The prolonged heat of an oven doesn't hurt them at all. Of course, they *can* ultimately be broken, but short of that, not much can ruin a clay pot.

Paul's leadership had those very same characteristics. He described his life of constant trials in 2 Corinthians 4:8–9: "We are hard pressed on every side, yet not crushed; we are perplexed, but not in despair; persecuted, but not forsaken; struck down, but not destroyed."

Yes, he was a clay pot—in some ways fragile, breakable, replaceable, valueless. But don't underestimate him, either. He was a *sturdy* clay pot, not eggshell china. This quality is absolutely essential to anyone in leadership: *A leader is resilient.*

This is a marvelous partner to the virtue of humility. The leader, while knowing his own weakness, must be strong and stalwart.

Leaders are perpetually beset with trials. After all, leadership is about people, and people cause problems. Some people *are* problems. The leader, while being fully cognizant of his own frailty, must nonetheless find strength to endure every kind of trial—including pressure, perplexity, persecution, and pain. Notice that Paul speaks of those very trials in a series of four vivid contrasts (hard pressed, not crushed; perplexed, not in despair; persecuted, not forsaken; struck down, not destroyed).

To those who charged that Paul's weaknesses crippled his ministry, he replied that he had been strong enough to endure every ordeal he had faced. Whatever did not kill him would only make him stronger. Paul (like a classic clay pot) was humble, yet durable. He was quite aware of all his own weaknesses. But at the same time, in those weaknesses he was mighty (cf. 2 Corinthians 12:10).

Nothing is more completely Christlike than that sort of strength in weakness. "Though He was crucified in weakness, yet He lives by the power of God. For we also are weak in Him, but we shall live with Him by the power of God toward you" (2 Corinthians 13:4). Again we see that the strength behind our resilience is *God's* power. The leader who is called and empowered by God and utterly dependent on Him for strength has infinite resources on which to draw. *Durable?* Such a leader is practically *invincible.*

Paul was not the sort of decorative pottery that sat on a shelf somewhere; he was a mercilessly battered jar. He was hammered all his life by people who would have been quite happy to see him break into a thousand pieces. The circumstances of his beleaguered life and transient ministry also added many hardships over and above the stress of dealing with people.

"The sufferings of Christ abound in us," he wrote (2 Corinthians 1:5).

"We were burdened beyond measure, above strength, so that we despaired even of life. Yes, we had the sentence of death in ourselves" (vv. 8–9). "But in all things we commend ourselves as ministers of God: in much patience, in tribulations, in needs, in distresses, in stripes, in imprisonments, in tumults, in labors, in sleeplessness, in fastings" (6:4–5).

This was nothing new for him. In his earlier epistle to the church at Corinth, he had written, "To the present hour we both hunger and thirst, and we are poorly clothed, and beaten, and homeless. And we labor, working with our own hands. Being reviled,

> **Leadership Principle #19**
> **A LEADER IS RESILIENT.**

we bless; being persecuted, we endure; being defamed, we entreat. We have been made as the filth of the world, the offscouring of all things until now" (1 Corinthians 4:11–13).

That was Paul's life. The trials were profound and seemingly endless:

From the Jews five times I received forty stripes minus one. Three times I was beaten with rods; once I was stoned; three times I was shipwrecked; a night and a day I have been in the deep; in journeys often, in perils of waters, in perils of robbers, in perils of my own countrymen, in perils of the Gentiles, in perils in the city, in perils in the wilderness, in perils in the sea, in perils among false brethren; in weariness and toil, in sleeplessness often, in hunger and thirst, in fastings often, in cold and nakedness. (2 Corinthians 11:24–27)

And, he added, "besides the other things, what comes upon me daily: my deep concern for all the churches" (v. 28).

All Paul ever really knew in his life was tribulation. But even though he was constantly assaulted, scraped and scoured, pressured, put in the flames, and otherwise abused, none of that could destroy him. He had a kind of invincible resilience, because the power of God was at work in him. His critics therefore were left having to face the undeniable impact of his life.

It was a powerful rebuttal. How could anyone explain the influence of Paul's life and ministry? How could they account for his zeal, his persistence, his durability, and his unwavering faithfulness? If Paul himself was weak and common (as the false apostles themselves were so eager to point out)—if he was merely a humble clay pot—then the only possible explanation for such a remarkable life was the power of God. This was undeniable proof that Paul was a true servant of God, and his accusers were false apostles.

CLAY POTS ARE EXPENDABLE

Because they cost little to produce and have no intrinsic value, clay pots are virtually disposable. As a clay-pot leader, Paul did not mind giving himself away. He did not fear death, slander, persecution, or suffering. He wrote, "[We are] always carrying about in the body the dying of the Lord Jesus, that the life of Jesus also may be manifested in our body. For we who live are always delivered to death for Jesus' sake, that the life of Jesus also may be manifested in our mortal flesh. So then death is working in us, but life in you" (2 Corinthians 4:10–12).

The preceding verses 8 and 9 were a short litany of the sufferings he endured. Verses 10–12 explain the significance of the suffering. Paul's mortal flesh—this inconsequential clay pot—was a kind of tureen from which the sufferings of Christ were continually being poured out. Thus Paul elevated his suffering to a lofty, noble, spiritual level. It was not really Paul whom the enemies of truth wanted to kill; it was the Lord Jesus. The same evil hatred that put Christ on the cross is still at work in the world, but now it pursues His faithful servants. Paul was bearing all that abuse daily—"always [being] delivered to death *for Jesus' sake*" (v. 11, emphasis added).

Notice the word *always*. There was no relief from the suffering. It was a kind of perpetual, daily death. In 1 Corinthians 15:31, he said, "I die daily." In Romans 8:36 he drew the same truth from Psalm 44:22: "We are killed all day long; we are accounted as sheep for the slaughter." In Galatians 6:17 he said, "I bear in my body the marks of the Lord Jesus."

Such suffering is inevitable for any leader who is faithful to Christ. Jesus gave a long discourse on this subject in Matthew 10: "Behold, I send you out as sheep in the midst of wolves" (v. 16). He reminded them, "A disciple is not above his teacher, nor a servant above his master. It is enough for a disciple that he be like his teacher, and a servant like his master. If they have called the master of the house Beelzebub, how much more will they call those of his household! *Therefore do not fear them*" (vv. 24–26, emphasis added). He went on to add, "Do not fear those who kill the body but cannot kill the soul. But rather fear Him who is able to destroy both soul and body in hell" (v. 28). In John 15:18–21, the Lord also told His disciples:

If the world hates you, you know that it hated Me before it hated you. If you were of the world, the world would love its own. Yet because you are not of the world, but I chose you out of the world, therefore the world hates you. Remember the word that I said to you, "A servant is not greater than his master." If they persecuted Me, they will also persecute you. If they kept My word, they will keep yours also. But all these things they will do to you for My name's sake, because they do not know Him who sent Me.

Paul told Timothy, "Yes, and all who desire to live godly in Christ Jesus will suffer persecution" (2 Timothy 3:12).

Walter Chalmers Smith, a poet, hymn writer, and minister in the Free Church of Scotland during the nineteenth century (author of the famous hymn "Immortal, Invisible, God Only Wise"), wrote these lines:

But all through life I see a cross
Where sons of God yield up their breath;
There is no gain except by loss,

> There is no life except by death,
> And no full vision but by faith,
> Nor glory, but by bearing shame,
> Nor justice, but by taking blame;
> And that Eternal Passion saith:
> Be emptied of glory, right and name.

That is a fitting manifesto for Christian leaders. Christ calls us all to the kind of sacrifice that is best characterized (the way Paul portrayed it) as perpetual dying.

Paul mentioned death some forty-five times in the New Testament. Normally, he used the Greek noun *thanatos*, which speaks of death as a fact. Here in 2 Corinthians 4:10, however, he uses a participle, *nekrosis* ("dying"), which speaks of the process of human mortality. Paul saw his whole life as a process of dying. He wasn't being morbid; he was simply recognizing the true nature of his earthly existence. It was a hopeful, not a gloomy, perspective: "To me, to live is Christ, and to die is gain" (Philippians 1:21).

As a mere clay pot, Paul knew he was expendable and was willing to be sacrificed. In Colossians 1:24, he wrote, "I now rejoice in my sufferings for you, and fill up in my flesh what is lacking in the afflictions of Christ, for the sake of His body, which is the church." He wasn't suggesting that Christ's sufferings weren't enough to purchase full redemption, or that Paul's own afflictions added something to the finished work of Christ's atonement. He did not imagine there was any saving merit in his pain. But, as he had already said in 2 Corinthians 1:5–6, his sufferings had a profound temporal benefit, even for the Corinthians: "As the sufferings of Christ abound in us, so our consolation also abounds through Christ. Now if we are afflicted, it is for your consolation and salvation, which is effective for enduring the same sufferings which we also suffer. Or if we are comforted, it is for your consolation and salvation."

In other words, his sacrifice was ultimately for their benefit. "So then death is working in us, but life in you" (4:12). "For all things are for your sakes, that grace, having spread through the many, may cause thanksgiving to abound to the glory of God" (v. 15). "Therefore I endure all things for the sake of the elect, that they also may obtain the salvation which is in Christ Jesus with eternal glory. This is a faithful saying: For if we died with Him, we shall also live with Him. If we endure, we shall also reign with Him" (2 Timothy 2:10–12). It wasn't some masochistic love of pain that drove Paul, but love for the Corinthians.

Nonetheless, as far as Paul was concerned, the trials were welcome. He expressed his main longing in Philippians 3:10: "that I may know [Christ] and the power of His resurrection, and the fellowship of His sufferings, being conformed to His death."

Remember that Jesus' earthly sufferings were not limited to the pains of the cross. He, too, was relentlessly stalked and ruthlessly hunted by His enemies. He lived in the face of death until He died on the cross. None of us will ever suffer a fraction of what He suffered. Few of us will be called upon to bear even a tenth as much hardship as Paul bore. But every leader who is faithful to Christ will have *some* share in His sufferings. The true leader must be willing to "endure hardship as a good soldier of Jesus Christ" (2 Timothy 2:3). It is a privilege to bear such things *for Christ's sake* (Romans 8:17–18). "Our light affliction, which is but for a moment, is working for us a far more exceeding and eternal weight of glory" (2 Corinthians 4:17).

When we learn to embrace trials, anguish, and distress as friends (James 1:2–4; Romans 5:3–5) and as reminders of our own weakness (2 Corinthians 12:7–10), we become more dependent on the power of God and therefore more effective as leaders and witnesses for Him. His life is unleashed in our dying. "I have been crucified with Christ," Paul wrote in Galatians 2:20. "It is no longer I who live, but Christ lives in me; and the life which I now live in the flesh I live by faith in the Son of God."

The testimony of such a life is powerful beyond measure. For Paul, the life of Jesus was being manifested in his own mortal flesh (2 Corinthians 4:11). Here was this battered, bruised, hammered, maligned, persecuted man, who was nothing but an earthenware vessel. But in his nothingness Christ's life was being manifested. How else could anyone explain the courage of Paul's preaching and the transformation of so many lives under his influence? Right there in Corinth, total pagans with no knowledge of the true God had come to faith in Christ after hearing Paul preach in their city square. What could account for that, other than the power of God?

Paul was exposed constantly to forces that were intent on killing him. Yet he was more than a conqueror (Romans 8:37), because the Lord Jesus Christ infused his life with such power that his influence as a spiritual leader overturned the world. The powerful influence of Paul's life and writings is still felt today, as it has been felt across the centuries.

He told the Corinthians, "I will very gladly spend and be spent for your souls" (2 Corinthians 12:15). To the Philippians, he likewise said, "Yes, and if I am being poured out as a drink offering on the sacrifice and service of your faith, I am glad and rejoice with you all" (Philippians 2:17). It was a worthy use for a disposable clay pot. Such a life of sacrifice suited Paul fine, because the return on the investment was so worthwhile.

Chapter Nine

THE LEADER'S WARFARE

The apostle Paul's relationship with the Corinthian church had been deliberately and systematically sabotaged by the false teachers' lies. Paul spent the first seven chapters of 2 Corinthians replying point by point to various things he knew had been said against him in Corinth. Interspersed in those chapters are a few doctrinal sections, but for the most part, those chapters are intensely personal, highly emotional, and thoroughly pastoral. Paul was seeking to repair the damaged relationship.

By the end of chapter 7, he seemed to have thoroughly unburdened himself. He closed that section with these words: "Therefore I rejoice that I have confidence in you in everything" (2 Corinthians 7:16). It reads like a great, sweeping, comprehensive sigh of relief.

Then for two chapters, he turned to the subject of the Corinthians' charity toward the church in Jerusalem. The saints in Judea were suffering greatly under the Roman persecution. The Macedonian churches, under Paul's leadership, had generously organized an offering to help meet the financial needs of their brethren in Judea (2 Corinthians 8:1–7). The Corinthians had offered to participate (vv. 10–11). Paul spent chapters 8–9 graciously encouraging them to fulfill that commitment. In those two chapters he was gentle, encouraging, and very mild in tone.

But then, as Paul began the closing section of his epistle (chapters 10–13), his whole demeanor seemed to change in an abrupt, marked, and surprising way. He became firm and militant. He included several pointed rebukes addressed directly and specifically to naive and disobedient people in the Corinthian church who had gullibly jumped on the false teachers' bandwagon (11:4, 19–21; 12:11; 13:2–3). For those reading the epistle who may have thought he was finished dealing with the threat of the false apostles, it turned out he had saved the harshest reproofs of all for the end.

In portions of this closing section of the epistle, Paul's language is *very* severe. Here is Paul at his most passionate, contending fiercely against those who were deceptively undermining his leadership.

At the beginning of the epistle, Paul had taken great care to make clear that his self-defense was not motivated by pride or egotism. He continued to make that clear, remarking again and again that every hint of boasting seemed utterly repugnant to him (10:8, 13–16; 11:10, 16–18, 30; 12:1, 5–6, 9, 11). And yet, no matter how humble Paul was, he would not blithely turn the Corinthians over to purveyors of lies. He was meek and modest, but he was by no means indifferent.

An apathetic leader is a contradiction in terms. No true leader will ever be uncaring. In fact, this is another fundamental principle of all leadership: *A leader is passionate.*

The person who is detached and indifferent is no true leader. All leaders must have passion, and spiritual leaders especially must be driven by an intense passion for the truth, as well as a deep, fervent, and abiding love for Christ. It is impossible to maintain such affections and be passive or unemotional.

In his classic work titled *Spiritual Leadership,* Oswald Sanders even included anger in his list of qualifications for leadership. He wrote:

> This sounds like a rather strange qualification for leadership. In another context it could be quoted as a disqualifying factor. But

was this quality not present in the life of the supreme Leader? "Jesus looked on them with anger" (John 2:15–17). Righteous wrath is no less noble than love, since both coexist in God. Each necessitates the other. It was Jesus' love for the man with the withered hand that aroused His anger against those who would deny him healing (Mark 3:5). It was His love for His Father, and zeal for His glory, that kindled His anger against the mercenary traders who had turned His house of prayer for all nations into a cave of robbers (Matthew 21:13).

Great leaders who have turned the tide in days of national and spiritual declension have been men who could get angry at the injustices and abuses which dishonor God and enslave men.[1]

Other strong affections as well—including joy, gladness, sorrow, compassion, fear, and love—are equally essential in leadership. The person who is cold, unfeeling, aloof, or apathetic can never be a truly effective leader.

Human passions, of course, pose certain hazards. They are subject to abuse and misuse. They can

> *Leadership Principle #20*
> **A LEADER IS PASSIONATE.**

severely cloud the rational faculties. Leaders, while never devoid of feeling or intensity, must harness their passions rather than being harnessed by them. Our zeal must be focused, carefully governed, and used for godly purposes. Self-control is a fruit of the Spirit (Galatians 5:23). Godly self-control involves not only the mortification of sinful lusts (Colossians 3:5), but also a degree of restraint in the expression of legitimate passions. Solomon wrote, "Whoever has no rule over his own spirit is like a city broken down, without walls" (Proverbs 25:28); and "He who is slow to anger is better than the mighty, and he who rules his spirit than he who takes a city" (16:32).

Nonetheless, there is "a time to weep, and a time to laugh; a time to mourn, and a time to dance . . . a time to love, and a time to hate; a time of war, and a time of peace" (Ecclesiastes 3:4, 8). The time for war had come against the lies of the false apostles, and Paul did not attempt to conceal his earnest passion as he concluded this second epistle to the church at Corinth. He even began that closing section by introducing a warfare motif:

> Now I, Paul, myself am pleading with you by the meekness and gentleness of Christ—who in presence am lowly among you, but being absent am bold toward you. But I beg you that when I am present I may not be bold with that confidence by which I intend to be bold against some, who think of us as if we walked according to the flesh. For though we walk in the flesh, we do not war according to the flesh. For the weapons of our warfare are not carnal but mighty in God for pulling down strongholds, casting down arguments and every high thing that exalts itself against the knowledge of God, bringing every thought into captivity to the obedience of Christ, and being ready to punish all disobedience when your obedience is fulfilled. (2 Corinthians 10:1–6)

In all the warfare the apostle endured—including various riots, stonings, and beatings from which he barely escaped with his life—nothing was more difficult or more relentless than the warfare he waged for the preservation of the Corinthian church. Little did Paul know during those first twenty months or so when he launched his ministry in Corinth that he would ultimately have to engage in a years-long battle just to preserve the truth of the gospel in that church.

But false teachers had come in almost as soon as Paul left. They had directly attacked Paul's leadership. And they achieved a shocking degree of success in turning that church against their founder and spiritual father.

Paul fought back. His epistles to the Corinthians pleaded for their repentance and expressed his deep love and abiding commitment to them (2 Corinthians 2:1–4). The biblical record seems to suggest that most in

Corinth *did* repent of their disloyalty. That is why Paul's heart was turned from despair to joy when Titus reported to him that the Corinthians had received his severe letter (the noncanonical rebuke he had apparently sent after 1 Corinthians but before 2 Corinthians) with sorrow and repentance (7:6–16). That was a major turning point and a great victory.

Nonetheless, it is significant that Paul's immediate response was to write 2 Corinthians—another long letter filled with pleas for repentance, gentle admonitions, words of correction, and even strong rebukes. The conflict was not yet over. Paul knew what every good leader knows: Rebellion always sows seeds for more rebellion.

We see this vividly in the Old Testament account of Korah's rebellion. Korah had stirred up the Israelites against Moses' leadership. They demanded that Moses step down. God himself judged Korah and his followers in the most vivid and immediate way: The ground opened up and swallowed them alive (Numbers 16:23–33). The people of Israel were eyewitnesses of what happened to Korah and his followers. They saw the ground miraculously open up, literally consume the rebels, and then close over them. They also saw fire from heaven incinerate 250 of Korah's closest followers (v. 35).

You might think such a dramatic judgment would put an end to rebellion in Israel forever. Far from it. The fires were still smoking and the ground was still settling when the next major rebellion broke out. And this time, it was even worse. The entire nation was swept up in it. Scripture says, "On *the next day* all the congregation of the children of Israel complained against Moses and Aaron, saying, 'You have killed the people of the LORD'" (v. 41, emphasis added). They blamed *Moses* for what had happened to Korah! God responded by sending a plague. Verse 49 says, "Those who died in the plague were fourteen thousand seven hundred, besides those who died in the Korah incident."

Paul knew that the false apostles' insurgency in Corinth had only been pushed underground, and it wasn't very deep. Or, to switch metaphors, Paul knew there were still some glowing embers from the fires of accusation against him. Somewhere in the church at Corinth, perhaps in some obscure corner, those smoldering sparks were ready to be fanned into flame at the first opportunity. The false teachers were still out there. Sympathies for the false teachers were apparently still being harbored by some in the congregation. The rebellion and the false teaching had merely gone into hiding, waiting for an opportune moment to break into the open again.

Paul further understood that the effects of slander are always long-lived. Once lies about you have been circulated, it is extremely difficult to clear your name. It's a lot like trying to recover dandelion seeds after they have been thrown to the wind. The lies against Paul had been devised with great cleverness and subtlety. They were mixed with just enough valid facts (cf. 2 Corinthians 10:9–10) to make them believable. They were disseminated by people who were convincingly disguised as truth messengers—"angel[s] of light" (11:13–14).

Paul knew the purveyors of those lies would continue the war they had begun against him. Even if forced underground, the false teachers would simply adopt guerrilla tactics and carry on the fight. They would in effect become spiritual terrorists.

Therefore Paul pulled no punches in this closing section of 2 Corinthians. He wanted to leave the Corinthians with some final words that revealed the depth of his passion. He wanted them to *know* that he regarded the conflict with the false teachers as nothing less than warfare. He wanted to warn anyone who might still be harboring sympathies for the bogus apostles that he was now coming to fulfill his promise of a personal visit (12:14; 13:1). He is not absolutely certain what to expect on his arrival in Corinth: "I fear lest, when I come, I shall not find you such as I wish" (12:20). But when he came, he would be armed for conflict if necessary. If rebellious people and false teachers were still causing problems when he got there, it was going to be all-out war (13:2).

Remember, Paul was their spiritual father (1 Corinthians 4:15). Therefore he spoke to them sternly, like a displeased parent. These closing chapters are an extended ultimatum to let them know that he was quite serious about all the things he had dealt with theretofore. His fatherly patience had been exhausted over these matters. He was prepared, if necessary, to execute some fatherly discipline. "I write to those who have sinned before, and to all the rest, that if I come again I will not spare" (13:2). He is prepared to "punish all disobedience" (10:6). So this was a fatherly warning to the Corinthians.

More critically, he had to remove the threat of the false apostles. He wanted them to know that he was coming back with weapons of warfare that were divinely powerful for pulling down their stronghold of lies. He planned to search out and destroy everything that exalted itself against the knowledge of God.

That was why he moved from the calm and tender pleadings of chapters 1–9 to strong, stern, authoritative words.

Titus would be delivering 2 Corinthians on Paul's behalf (8:16–24). Sometime shortly after they received the letter, Paul himself would come for his third visit. He was already preparing for the journey (12:14). So they would have some time after reading the epistle to get ready for the apostle's coming. They needed to use that time to deal with the issues Paul raised in the epistle. Those who still might be on the fence needed to repent.

In effect, the closing four chapters of 2 Corinthians echo and expand on what Paul wrote in 1 Corinthians 4:21: "What do you want? Shall I come to you with a rod, or in love and a spirit of gentleness?" It was up to the Corinthians. And if things were already *that* urgent when Paul wrote his first epistle, they were more so now.

Paul had three groups of people in mind as he penned this portion of his letter. There were the faithful Corinthians, who had now reaffirmed their commitment to Paul. There were some fence-sitters, who apparently retained sympathies with the false apostles and wanted to remain undecided. And then there were the accusers themselves. Paul knew they still posed a great threat.

Paul's response to all three groups reveals the depth and range of his passion. He addressed the faithful ones with gentle, heartfelt compassion.

He cautioned the fence-sitters sternly and with boldness. And he militantly put his accusers on notice that they were not safe. All three of these are seen clearly in those first 6 verses of 2 Corinthians 10.

HIS COMPASSION

Paul was about to employ some powerful and militant language in verses 3–6. So in order to put that in its proper context, he began with an expression of tender, heartfelt compassion: "Now I, Paul, myself am pleading with you by the meekness and gentleness of Christ" (v. 1).

Paul knew, of course, that being misrepresented, slandered, reviled, persecuted, and wrongfully accused is an inevitable part of being a Christian. We must expect to suffer unjustly. Our lives confront the culture we live in. We live as aliens in the world, and it should not surprise us when the world is hostile toward us (1 John 3:13). We were called for that purpose. In this world we will have tribulation (John 16:33). It goes with the territory.

But remember that Paul's authority had been placed in dispute by the false teachers. His right to speak for God had been questioned. His apostolic credentials had been brought under attack. This was not merely a personal offense against Paul; it was a full-on assault against truth itself.

Paul had already thoroughly answered the challenge to his apostolic credentials. He had established the fact that he needed no letters of commendation to justify wielding the power of apostolic leadership over them (2 Corinthians 3:1). So here he began by clearly and forcefully putting himself in the place of authority. What he was about to say would be said with his full authority as an apostle of Jesus Christ—"I, Paul, myself." He was invoking the authority of his office.

And yet, even as he did so, it was with deliberate gentleness and meekness ("pleading with you by the meekness and gentleness of Christ"). He had no desire for conflict. He got no satisfaction out of combat. He was not motivated by venom or vitriol or anger. He recognized that the Corinthians had been deceived and misled, and he had reason to believe most of them were repentant. So he assured them that what he was about to say came from a heart filled with compassion, meekness, and tenderness toward them. He was certainly not looking for a war with *the church* in Corinth.

"Meekness" is a humble attitude that expresses itself in the patient endurance of offenses. Paul was free from all bitterness. He had no thirst for vengeance. "Gentleness" is virtually a synonym. It implies leniency and long-suffering. Paul had no malice or ill will toward the Corinthians. Rather, he was saying that the attitude of his heart toward them was a faithful mirror of Christ's own compassion ("the meekness and gentleness *of Christ*").

Meekness is not *weakness;* it is power under control. After all, no one was more powerful than Christ; yet He said, "I am gentle and lowly in heart" (Matthew 11:29). Paul likewise was keeping his apostolic authority in check. He was not looking for an opportunity to brandish his authority like a club. It was not in his heart to punish the Corinthians. He would do so if he had to, but that would be his last choice.

Jesus Himself exemplified that kind of patience, and all Christians are commanded to follow His example. Peter wrote:

This is commendable, if because of conscience toward God one endures grief, suffering wrongfully. For what credit is it if, when you are beaten for your faults, you take it patiently? But when you do good and suffer, if you take it patiently, this is commendable before God. For to this you were called, because Christ also suffered for us, leaving us an example, that you should follow His steps: "Who committed no sin, nor was deceit found in His mouth"; who, when He was reviled, did not revile in return; when He suffered, He did not threaten, but committed Himself to Him who judges righteously. (1 Peter 2:19–23)

No one in the world ever suffered more unjustly than Christ. He was sinless, totally innocent, completely without deceit. And yet when He was reviled, He did not return the taunts.

How merciful was Christ? Isaiah spoke of Him prophetically, saying, "A bruised reed He will not break, and smoking flax He will not quench" (Isaiah 42:3; cf. Matthew 12:20).

What does that mean? The reed was a stiff, canelike plant that grew near shallow water. Shepherds would whittle reeds into simple musical pipes. When a reed pipe became damaged, or "bruised," the shepherd would snap it in two, discard it, and make a new one. "Smoking flax" spoke of a burned-out lamp wick, worthless for giving light. Both represent something useless, something anyone would normally just throw away. But Christ's ministry was to redeem people who were otherwise worthless, not destroy and discard them. Such compassion set the spirit for His entire earthly mission (cf. Luke 9:51–56; 19:10; John 8:10–11). "God did not send His Son into the world to condemn the world, but that the world through Him might be saved" (John 3:17; cf. John 12:47).

Remember that even Jesus' most scathing denunciation—a blistering diatribe against the religious leaders of Jerusalem in Matthew 23—ends with Christ weeping over Jerusalem (v. 37). Compassion colored everything He did.

Paul said, in effect, "I come to you with the meekness and gentleness of Christ. I am willing to be patient. I want to be gentle and lenient. I have no anger or malice toward you." The Corinthians knew that was an expression of his true heart, because they knew the apostle so well.

But Paul's enemies had also observed his meekness, and they had already tried to put a negative spin on it. They claimed Paul seemed gentle only because he lacked real courage. He pretended to be bold from a distance. But in person he was gutless. Face-to-face, he was a wimp. As we observed in the previous chapter, they said, "His letters . . . are weighty and powerful, but his bodily presence is weak" (2 Corinthians 10:10).

They were saying, in effect, that he was like a dog behind the gate that barks its head off, but when you open the gate it runs the other direction. "Get Paul far enough away and put a pen in his hand and he becomes fierce. Bring him here and he's weak; he lacks courage."

They had misconstrued both his boldness and his compassion. It was a very clever accusation, because it was hard to answer by a letter. If he tried to defend his strength from a distance, they could say he made their point. If he wrote them a gentle reply, they would say *that* showed they were right about his "weakness."

So instead, he acknowledged the accusation, but only in a sarcastic throwaway line. (In effect, he more or less dismissed the charge without responding to it directly in so many words.) "I, Paul . . . who in presence am lowly among you, but being absent am bold toward you" (10:1). Then he replied in a way that welded his strength and his tenderness together. He began with a clear expression of compassion, but then he immediately began to speak with a calm firmness that soon rose to a militant tone. The note of gentle sarcasm signaled the shift from compassion to firmness.

HIS BOLDNESS

Then his attention was turned to the fence-sitters, those who had shown sympathies with the false apostles and who were, perhaps, still undecided about how to respond to Paul.

If they believed the false teachers' lies and mistook Paul for a coward, they were about to receive a rude awakening. He was not weak. If all his compassionate overtures were rejected, he was prepared to show them how bold he could be in person: "I beg you that when I am present I may not be bold with that confidence by which I intend to be bold against some, who think of us as if we walked according to the flesh" (2 Corinthians 10:2). The New International Version translates that verse like this: "I beg you that when I come I may not have to be as bold as I expect to be toward some people who think that we live by the standards of this world."

When Paul's efforts at patience were exhausted, he would do whatever was necessary to defend the truth against these unrepentant, unrelenting rebels. If *only* confrontation would preserve the truth, Paul would not back down from it. Indeed, he said he *expected* that would be the case with some. If they wanted severity, they would get it.

By the way, Paul was *not* always meek in face-to-face situations. Remember, on one occasion, he even rebuked *Peter.* He did it publicly, and "to his face, because he was to be blamed" (Galatians 2:11).

The record of Paul's personal courage fills the book of Acts, starting with chapter 13. He boldly stood against courts, councils, religious leaders, mobs, governors, kings, and especially false teachers. He was by no means weak or cowardly. That would have violated one of the cardinal principles of leadership: *A leader is courageous.*

No one who lacks the courage of basic convictions can possibly be an effective leader. People don't follow cowards. At times, the leader's courage is expressed in confrontation. That is the case here.

We have seen Paul's courage in action throughout our study. Now it comes into the center of our focus, as he replied to this ridiculous false allegation that he was too timid to be firm in face-to-face situations.

As we saw in the previous chapter, Paul's enemies had also complained that he had physical weaknesses and no oratorical elegance. Paul had simply acknowledged the truth of *those* charges. But *this* claim that he lacked courage was a flat-out lie. Paul exemplified fearlessness. Not once in the biblical record does he ever show an ounce of cowardice. No wonder he became indignant as he pondered how to answer this foolish accusation.

"God has not given us a spirit of fear, but of power and of love and of a sound mind," he told Timothy (2 Timothy 1:7). *Timothy* evidently struggled with a lack of bravery, because Paul frequently admonished him to be strong and not to be ashamed or timid (1:8; 2:1, 3; 1 Timothy 1:18; 6:12).

But Paul himself never showed any sign of fear or shyness. In fact, his courage moved dramatically to the forefront here in 2 Corinthians 10:2 as he answered his critics. He warned them that he fully "intend[ed] to be bold against some." The Greek word translated "bold" is *tolmao,* which means "to be courageous, daring, dauntless." It speaks of acting without fear of the consequences.

If they really wanted to see Paul's courage, he would show it. And he would do so "with . . . confidence." That expression translates the Greek word *tharrheo*, which is a close synonym for *courage*.

There was a clear crescendo in his tone as he wrote. He was becoming more aggressive. If the false teachers or their followers wanted a fight, he would give them a fight. "If I come again I will not spare" (13:2).

At this point, Paul gave insight into the true nature of the false teachers' accusations. They had caused people to "think of us as if we walked according to the flesh" (2 Corinthians 10:2). They were apparently claiming Paul was controlled by sinful desires. That is precisely what it means to "walk according to the flesh" (cf. Romans 8:1, 5).

> **Leadership Principle #21**
> **A LEADER IS COURAGEOUS.**

Paul elsewhere wrote, "The works of the flesh are evident, which are: adultery, fornication, uncleanness, lewdness, idolatry, sorcery, hatred, contentions, jealousies, outbursts of wrath, selfish ambitions, dissensions, heresies, envy, murders, drunkenness, revelries, and the like" (Galatians 5:19–21). Apparently, the false apostles' *specific* claim was that Paul was driven by the love of money (2 Corinthians 11:9–13; 12:13–19)—or perhaps even filthier lusts. They wanted the Corinthians to think Paul was utterly disqualified from spiritual leadership (13:6–7).

This takes us to the very heart of the conspiracy against Paul. Here is what lay at the very core of all the falsehoods. Every accusation, every insinuation, and every defamation they had tried to smear Paul with was merely a way to buttress this suspicion that he was a fraud who was morally bankrupt and driven by fleshly lusts. Paul's enemies had deliberately planted that suspicion. It had no basis whatsoever in any facts.

Paul had already defended himself against that lie. In 1:12, you'll recall, he practically started off the whole epistle by saying, "Our boasting is this: the testimony of our conscience that we conducted ourselves in the world in simplicity and godly sincerity." In 7:2, he said, "We have wronged no one, we have corrupted no one, we have cheated no one." Thus he had answered the slander without dignifying it with any explicit recognition.

But now he brings the accusation out and lays it on the table for all to see. Lest anyone imagine that he was overreacting, here is what had aroused such boldness in him. This was the real gist of the attacks on him: They had falsely portrayed Paul as a phony, mercenary, Elmer Gantry–type minister. They claimed he was motivated purely by self-interest, corrupt desires, fleshly lusts, and secret motives.

Paul didn't want to be harsh. He was not looking for conflict. But unless the rebels who invented such wicked falsehoods repented or left before Paul arrived, it would be war. He promised.

HIS MILITANCY

Thus Paul's rising intensity finally culminated in an all-out declaration of war. The leader's compassion doesn't cancel out his willingness to fight. His courage is equal to his passion.

Paul's enemies had accused him of walking "according to the flesh" (2 Corinthians 10:2)—in a fleshly manner. He flatly and forcefully denied the accusation that he was morally corrupt. He also threatened to display his boldness against anyone who impugned his character in that way. Nonetheless, in verse 3, he acknowledged that there was a *true* sense in which he "walk[ed] in the flesh"—he was, after all, a mortal, made of human flesh. He was making a play on words. He still denied, of course, that he walked "according to the flesh" in the moral sense. But he also admitted that he was still "in the flesh" in the human sense. In other words, he wasn't claiming to be supernatural.

And yet he was prepared to wage war in the supernatural realm. He said, "Though we walk in the flesh, we do not war according to the flesh. For the weapons of our warfare are not carnal but mighty in God for pulling down strongholds, casting down arguments and every high thing that exalts itself against the knowledge of God, bringing every thought into captivity to the obedience of Christ" (vv. 3–5).

This is an amazingly bold challenge to the enemies of truth. In effect,

Paul was saying, "You want to go to war with me? *Throw down.* But let me warn you, when you look at me, all you see is a mortal man. But when we go to battle, I won't be using human weapons. I won't fight on your level. I won't use conventional human weapons." It was war on another plane. Paul fought "by the word of truth, by the power of God, by the armor of righteousness on the right hand and on the left" (2 Corinthians 6:7).

Paul knew the real battle was not merely against the human false teachers who had confused the Corinthians. It was nothing less than full-scale war against the kingdom of darkness. "We do not wrestle against flesh and blood, but against principalities, against powers, against the rulers of the darkness of this age, against spiritual hosts of wickedness in the heavenly places" (Ephesians 6:12). We are fighting for the preservation and proclamation of the *truth.* We are fighting for the honor of Jesus Christ. We are fighting for the salvation of sinners, and we are fighting for the virtue of saints.

In fact, for every good and noble effort of Christian leaders in business, politics, education, the military, or any other legitimate pursuit, there is inevitable engagement with the kingdom of darkness. Since all Christians, in whatever they do, are supposed to be engaged in the advance of Christ's kingdom, they face opposition from the powers of evil.

Paul used the language of warfare all the time. He began and ended 1 Timothy by urging Timothy to fight the battle well: "Wage the good warfare" (1:18); "Fight the good fight of faith" (6:12). He said, "Be sober, putting on the breastplate of faith and love, and as a helmet the hope of salvation" (1 Thessalonians 5:8). In 2 Timothy 2:3 he said, "Endure hardship as a good soldier of Jesus Christ." As Paul himself neared the end of his own life, he wrote, "I have fought the good fight" (2 Timothy 4:7). His whole life was a spiritual war against anything and everything that opposed the truth.

You cannot fight on that level with human weapons. Carnal tools have no power whatsoever against the kingdom of darkness. The most powerful human arsenal is totally impotent against principalities and powers, against the rulers of the darkness of this world, or against spiritual wickedness in the heavenlies. Fleshly instruments can't fight on that level. Human weapons have no power at all against Satan. They cannot liberate souls from the kingdom of darkness. They cannot transform sinners. They cannot sanctify saints. They have no effect in the spiritual realm or the kingdom of darkness.

What did Paul mean by "carnal" weapons? Obviously, he would include every instrument used in literal human warfare. Paul wasn't literally planning an incursion with swords and chariots into the camp of the enemy. He wasn't actually thinking of using physical force in Corinth.

But a moment's reflection will reveal that every type of worldly device and human invention that has ever been brought into battle against the powers of darkness is also merely a different kind of fleshly weapon. That would include human philosophy, rationalistic arguments, carnal strategy, fleshly ingenuity, human cleverness, entertainment, showmanship, and every other innovation that is supposed to augment the power of the gospel. Such strategies are in full fashion these days. But all of them are impotent weapons. They represent vain attempts to fight spiritual battles on a human level.

You can use such gimmicks to sell soup and Chevrolets. You can employ them in political campaigns or for public-relations purposes. But in spiritual warfare they are utterly useless. They're like plastic popguns with Ping-Pong balls. They can never be truly effective against the fortresses of the evil one. Even if your job is to sell cars or food products, if you are a Christian, you are a soldier in a spiritual battle, and for that battle, you need to be skilled in the use of the right weapons.

Paul said the weapons he took to battle were "mighty in God" (2 Corinthians 10:4); "divinely powerful" (NASB). He was saying these were weapons that came from heaven—from God's own personal arsenal. He certainly was not talking about gimmicks and novelties designed to make his message more marketable. What Paul had in mind were clearly not weapons of human invention, but divinely ordained, spiritually powerful weapons.

Why? Because the enemy is formidable and, frankly, gimmicks and human cleverness won't do what needs to be done. We need divinely powerful weapons "for pulling down strongholds" (v. 4). The spiritual fortresses Paul was describing are impervious to fleshly weapons.

The Corinthians would have had a clear picture in their minds when Paul mentioned "strongholds." Just to the south of their city and towering over it was a massive mountain, a natural tower of rock more than eighteen hundred feet high, known as Acrocorinthus. On it stood an impregnable fortress, flanked by the Temple of Aphrodite. From that elevated citadel, the acropolis of Athens was visible more than forty-five miles away. The fortress atop Acrocorinthus was where the entire population of Corinth would retreat in case of an attack. From there they could easily defend themselves. They knew the strategic value of that fortress. It was a massive, high bulwark that could not easily be overthrown. In fact, it still towers over the ruins of Corinth today.

Paul said the spiritual strongholds of the powers of darkness are similar to that—except they are spiritual and supernatural. Such fortifications obviously cannot be assaulted with worldly weapons.

Notice also that Paul's strategy was not merely to lob a few shots at the fortresses, but to demolish them. The expression "pulling down strongholds" speaks of utterly bringing them to ruin, causing them to crumble and disintegrate.

What are these fortresses? What, actually, was Paul attacking? He gave the answer very clearly in verse 5: "Casting down arguments and every high thing that exalts itself against the knowledge of God." The New American Standard Bible speaks of "destroying speculations." The King James Version says, "Casting down imaginations." The Greek word is *logismos*, which signifies opinions, calculations, or reasonings. The only other place the word is found in the New Testament is in Romans 2:15, where it is translated "thoughts" and describes the process of rationalizing in order to make an excuse.

In other words, the fortresses Paul was describing are corrupt belief systems, sinister philosophies, false doctrines, evil worldviews, and every massive system of falsehood. Obviously, if we are in a battle for truth, the fortresses we need to demolish are the bastions of *lies*—wrong thoughts, wicked ideas, untrue opinions, immoral theories, and false religions. These are *ideological* forts—philosophical forts, religious forts—spiritual strongholds made of thoughts, ideas, concepts, opinions. In such ideological citadels, sinful people try to hide and fortify themselves against God and against the gospel of Christ.

Spiritual warfare as Paul described it is therefore ideological rather than mystical. Our enemies are demonic, but the warfare against them isn't waged by commanding them, mapping their physical location, invoking magic words to subdue them, claiming authority over them, or any of the other common tactics some people usually refer to as "spiritual warfare." We are not fighting demons in a face-to-face confrontation, or by spirit-to-spirit conversation, or with voice-to-voice communication. We attack them by tearing down their fortresses of lies.

The enemy has devised massive citadels of falsehood. We assault those ideologies. Our war is against "deceiving spirits and doctrines of demons" (1 Timothy 4:1). We wage that war by attacking the demons' elaborately constructed systems of lies—by tearing down the fortresses, not by trying to command the spirits themselves.

In 1 Corinthians 3:19–20 the enemy fortresses are called "the wisdom of this world" and "the thoughts of the wise." These are the various thought systems people have raised up against the knowledge of God. Romans 1 describes the course humanity has followed into sin. Although the truth of God's existence and infinite power are clearly visible in creation (Romans 1:20), sinful humanity has turned against God, suppressed the knowledge of Him, embraced foolish and futile thoughts instead, and "exchanged the truth of God for the lie" (vv. 21–25). Every worldly ideology that opposes God, opposes Christ, and opposes the Bible is rooted in that same rebellion and spawned out of hell. That is what we wage war against. False religions. Humanistic philosophies. Secular rationalism. Those are the high things that exalt themselves

against the knowledge of God (2 Corinthians 10:5). And they have to
be brought down.

That brings up a crucial question: What, precisely, are our weapons?
If the fortresses are constructed of "arguments and every high thing that
exalts itself against the knowledge of God" (v. 5; thoughts, concepts, opinions, ideologies, philosophies), it seems obvious that the only power that
will destroy such things is the power of *truth*. Indeed, when the apostle
Paul listed the armor of spiritual warfare in Ephesians 6:13–17, he named
only one offensive weapon in the panoply: "the sword of the Spirit, which
is the word of God" (v. 17). The power of God for salvation is the power
of the gospel alone (Romans 1:16; cf. 1 Corinthians 1:21).

In other words, "the weapons of our warfare" are the instruments of truth.
The Word of God. The gospel. Sound doctrine. The truth of Scripture.

The simple fact is that you can't fight spiritual warfare with magic
phrases and secret words. You don't overpower demons merely by shout-
ing at them. I don't have anything to say to a demon anyway. I'm not
interested in talking to them. Let the Lord do that (cf. Jude 9). Why
would I even want to communicate with evil spirits? But I have a lot to
say to people who have barricaded themselves in fortresses of demonic lies.
I want to do everything I can to tear down those palaces of lies. And the
only thing that equips me to do that well is the Word of God.

Spiritual warfare is all about demolishing evil lies with the truth. Use
the authority of God's Word and the power of the gospel to give people the
truth. That is what will pull
down the fortresses of falsehood. That is the real nature
of spiritual warfare. That is

> *Leadership Principle #22*
> **A LEADER IS DISCERNING.**

precisely what Paul described here in 2 Corinthians 10.

What does all this have to do with leadership? One of the fundamental qualifications for spiritual leadership is a knowledge of the truth,
an ability to recognize lies, and skill in using the truth to refute the lies.
A leader is discerning.

One of the key requirements Paul listed for elders in the church was that they have to be skilled enough with the Word of God to "be able, by sound doctrine, both to exhort and convict those who contradict" (Titus 1:9). One who is not able to engage in the spiritual warfare on this level is simply not equipped to lead well.

Furthermore, you cannot be a good leader and *avoid* the warfare. As Paul's life demonstrated, the more effective you are as a leader, the more the enemy will bring the battle to you. That is the nature of leadership. We therefore cannot lead well or fight the battle well unless we learn the Scriptures and acquire skill in using God's truth to answer lies.

Lies yield only to the truth. Rebellion ends when truth prevails. If you're a leader who is also a Christian, you may not realize it, but you are engaged in spiritual warfare. You need to be armed. You need to know the Word of God. And you need to develop skill in using it against the lies of the evil one.

PART 3

AN APPROVED WORKMAN: LEADERSHIP HELD TO A BIBLICAL STANDARD

Chapter Ten

HOW NOT TO
BE DISQUALIFIED

I n these final chapters, we will look at what qualifies a leader to lead. We begin, however, by looking at a common pitfall that can easily *disqualify* a person from leadership even after he has made a good start. This is the one snare that has probably caused the downfall of more leaders than any other hazard: a lack of personal discipline.

Naturally gifted people sometimes find it hard to maintain discipline. The musician who has superior skill might perform well without a lot of practice. The talented athlete might play well without working as hard as his teammates. An artist with extraordinary abilities might not have to work very hard to excel. For that reason, some of the most talented individuals in the world are also the most undisciplined. We frequently see shocking evidence of this in the lifestyles of celebrities and sports heroes.

Paul was a supremely gifted natural leader. We can deduce that from the fact that even as a young man, he was given oversight of the Sanhedrin's campaign against Christians (Acts 7:58). In Acts 26:10, recounting his fierce opposition to the gospel before he met Christ, he said, "Many of the saints I shut up in prison, having received authority from the chief priests;

and when they were put to death, I cast my vote against them." The fact that he could cast a vote strongly suggests that he himself was probably a member of the Sanhedrin, the highest ruling council in all Judaism.

To attain such stature at so young an age speaks of an amazing intellect and superior gifts. And yet we have already seen abundant proof that the apostle Paul was not one to rest on his own natural abilities, intellectual prowess, or leadership gifts. "I labored more abundantly than they all," he said in 1 Corinthians 15:10, "yet not I, but the grace of God which was with me."

And thus Paul highlighted for us another critical, indispensable, and supremely important quality every leader must maintain: *A leader is disciplined.*

Self-control is absolutely vital to lasting success in any endeavor of life. Many people do attain a degree of prominence on the strength of sheer natural talent alone. But the real, influential *leaders* are the ones who devote themselves to personal discipline and make the most of their gifts. Those who utterly lack self-control will invariably fail, and they forfeit the example of integrity so essential to the best kind of true leadership.

The apostle Paul, as we have already seen many times, was absolutely certain of his calling. He confidently defended his apostleship when others attacked his authority. He had no doubt whatsoever about his rightful place as a leader. After all, he was called in an extraordinary way to a unique role. Paul indicated that the risen Christ even appeared to him in physical form (1 Corinthians 15:8; cf. Acts 23:11). In fact, Paul's face-to-face encounter with the glorified Lord was so remarkable and so singular that he pointed to it in defense of his apostleship (1 Corinthians 9:1). Paul also had the same ability Jesus gave the Twelve to work miracles, signs, and wonders (2 Corinthians 12:12; cf. Matthew 10:1).

No wonder Paul was so sure of his calling. God had specifically singled him out and ordained him to his missionary role and his apostolic office. God's calling and approval of Paul was made clear to all. In fact, Paul's apostolic commission was repeatedly confirmed in so many powerful and dramatic ways that even the most determined efforts of numerous scheming false apostles could not succeed in disqualifying him.

And yet Paul himself spoke with great apprehension about the possibility that he might yet be disqualified.

We might expect Paul to be so confident in his calling that he would never entertain any fear of ultimate failure. Shouldn't Paul of all people be immune from anxiety about the risk of being declared ineligible? But he wrote about that very concern in the most honest and explicit way.

> *Leadership Principle #23*
> A LEADER IS DISCIPLINED.

Paul often portrayed life as an athletic competition like the running of a race (Acts 20:24; Galatians 2:2; 5:7; Philippians 2:16; 3:13–14; 2 Timothy 2:5). He was determined to win the race. He did not want to stumble or collapse before reaching the finish line. In 1 Corinthians 9:24–27, he wrote these words, which give wonderful insight into the heart of a true leader:

> Do you not know that those who run in a race all run, but one receives the prize? Run in such a way that you may obtain it. And everyone who competes for the prize is temperate in all things. Now they do it to obtain a perishable crown, but we for an imperishable crown. Therefore I run thus: not with uncertainty. Thus I fight: not as one who beats the air. But I discipline my body and bring it into subjection, lest, when I have preached to others, I myself should become disqualified.

The Greek word translated "disqualified" in verse 27 is *adokimos*. It speaks of being rejected, eliminated by a rule violation, disapproved. It's the same word translated "reprobate" in the King James Version of Romans 1:28 ("God gave them over to a reprobate mind"). Paul was describing the sort of shameful, disgraceful, personal elimination that occurs when an athlete is found to have deliberately cheated or otherwise violated the rules of the race.

Obviously, Paul had no fear that his enemies might disqualify him by their attacks on his apostolic credentials. He weathered all such attacks with supreme confidence and conviction, as we have already observed. But here he was talking about an entirely different kind of disqualification. He was saying he did not want to render *himself* ineligible. He did not want to crash and burn morally and be spiritually disqualified.

This is a grave danger for all in leadership. The leader's confidence in his own calling must be matched and balanced by a holy dread of personal spiritual failure. Leaders are exposed to unique and singular temptations. Because of the critical role they play, they face extraordinary attacks from the powers of darkness. Pride has been a peculiar snare for many; a lack of purity and self-control has caused others to founder. Moral and personal default has been the downfall of many in leadership. It all stems from a lack of discipline.

Samson's strength was overcome because of his own lack of self-control. Solomon's wisdom was compromised by his lust. And if David, a man after God's own heart, could succumb to the lust of the eyes and commit adultery and murder, no leader ever ought to feel immune from personal failure. Paul certainly did not.

As a matter of fact, that was Paul's one great concern about his own role as a leader. He did not want to disqualify himself from the race. Therefore he disciplined himself, restrained his fleshly desires, and brought his own body into subjection, so that the time would never come, after having preached to others, when he himself would be disqualified. He kept his eye on the prize (Philippians 3:13–14). He exercised himself unto godliness (1 Timothy 4:7). And he ran the race with endurance (Hebrews 12:1).

COMPETING FOR THE PRIZE

Why run a race at all, unless you're running to win? No true competitor wants to finish second.

These days we have lots of "fun runs" and marathons that attract thousands of amateur runners whose only goal is to finish the race. The prize they are seeking to attain is the satisfaction of completing the race (sometimes whether they finish *well* or not). There's nothing wrong with that in a race for pure recreation. But in a real athletic competition, the goal is to win. And Paul portrayed all of life and ministry as a real competition, not a fun run. He took the contest seriously, and he lived accordingly.

The Corinthians understood athletic competition as well as any modern ESPN junkie. Since the time of Alexander the Great, athletics had dominated Greek society. The two most important athletic events were the Olympic Games held every fourth year in Athens, and the Isthmian games held every other year (in the spring of the second and fourth years of the Olympiad) in Corinth. The Isthmian games were among the most famous attractions of the city. Everyone in Corinth knew something about athletics.

And one thing everyone knew was that in order to get the prize, you had to win the race. In the Isthmian games, the prize was a wreath made of pine leaves. But along with that came fame and high honor. Winners were venerated above all others in society, exactly as our society does with sports heroes today. Every young man in Corinth dreamed of winning the prize.

I was an athlete in high school and college. I was on the football, baseball, and track teams. I *always* competed to win. That was my whole life in those days. And I was able to achieve a moderate degree of athletic success. When I think of the sacrifices I was willing to make to run on a football field with a piece of pig under my arm, it seems almost inconceivable to me today.

Notice what Paul said about earthly athletes: "They do it to obtain a perishable crown" (1 Corinthians 9:25). A pine wreath. Something that was not even comfortable hanging around the winner's neck. These days, the most prestigious prize for a runner is an Olympic gold medal. I'm told the material from which they are made is worth about $110. These are perishable prizes. They have little intrinsic value. Even the intangible rewards are short-lived. And yet athletes make amazing sacrifices to win them.

When I was in college, school athletes were paid nothing. At my school there were not even any amenities that went along with an athletic scholarship. But there was a record board in the school gymnasium, and it was every athlete's wish to get his name on that board.

I had a decent career in college football and was able to set a few school records. I remember going into the gymnasium when I graduated from college and looking at that record board. My name was there in multiple categories in the various sports I had played. It seemed like a big deal at the time.

But then just a year later I returned for an alumni event, and I looked at the board and noticed that several of my records had already been broken. That would have been heartrending enough, but when I came back a few years later, the board was gone. Not long afterward, the school went out of existence. The final blow to my glory as an athlete came in 1971, when a major earthquake shook my football trophy off a shelf and broke it beyond repair. My wife, Patricia, swept up the pieces and unceremoniously put them out with the trash.

Earthly accolades are fleeting and transitory. And yet athletes are willing to make amazing, long-term, hard-core sacrifices in order to achieve the prize.

Paul said if the worldly athlete is willing to discipline himself to win a pine wreath, what price would you pay to attain "an imperishable crown" (v. 25)—one that is "incorruptible and undefiled and that does not fade away" (1 Peter 1:4)?

Paul described his own quest for that prize in Philippians 3:13–14: "I do not count myself to have apprehended; but one thing I do, forgetting those things which are behind and reaching forward to those things which are ahead, I press toward the goal for the prize of the upward call of God in Christ Jesus." The race was not over. He had not yet achieved that which he strived for. He was determined not to stop short of the goal. To look back or look around would only slow him down unnecessarily. He therefore kept his objective in view and pressed on toward the prize. That is what every runner must do.

During college I ran the mile relay. One of our most important races of the year came at the Orange County Invitational. There were some thirty-five colleges and universities represented, and our team managed to get into the finals.

It was a four-man team. The first man needed to be a strong runner. His role was to get the lead early. The second man was the least strategic. If he lost the lead, we had two runners to make it up. So the third and fourth runners both had to be fast and durable. I was essentially a football player added to round out the track team, so I ran the second leg.

In this particular race, our first man ran a great leg and handed me the baton with a perfect pass. I ran the race of my life and managed to finish my lap in a dead heat for first place. I made a perfect baton pass to the third guy, who took off from there, already gaining on the competition. Our fourth man was unbeatable, so at that point, it looked as though we had the race won.

But as we watched the third man round out of the back stretch, he suddenly slowed, stopped, walked off the track, and sat on the infield. The race kept going. Of course, we were out of it. I was horrified, and so were the other guys on the team. We thought our third man had pulled a hamstring or something.

We ran across the infield grass to where he was sitting, nonchalantly adjusting his socks. "What happened? What happened?" we shouted.

I'll never forget his reply: "I don't know; I just didn't feel like running anymore."

I confess that my thoughts were pretty carnal at that moment. We were ready to annihilate him. We had wanted to win! We had our eyes on the prize. It was within reach. How could someone who had trained and worked hard to get in the race decide at *that* moment that he just didn't feel like running anymore—and let a whole team and school down? He obviously wasn't a leader.

I've observed over the years that all gifted leaders seem to have an innate drive to win. Those who lack the winning instinct don't make very effective leaders.

But if we are going to win *this* race, it will come at a price, or we will be disqualified.

TRAINING FOR THE CONTEST

The price of victory is discipline. That means self-control, sacrifice, and hard work. Athletes in Paul's day trained hard just to be able to compete in the competition. In order to enter the Isthmian games, athletes had to give proof of ten months' full-time training. For thirty days before the event, the athletes trained together daily, in public view. They followed a staggering regimen of exercise and discipline that eliminated all but the most devoted. Then, as now, it was a serious commitment to be a world-class athlete.

That was precisely how Paul portrayed the discipline he followed as a leader of God's people. This was no mere game to him. He was more serious than any track-and-field athlete. He wanted to win a race that had far more significance than any arena sport. Therefore it required even more diligence and discipline.

"Everyone who competes for the prize is temperate [moderate, self-restrained, not given to excess] in all things," he said in 1 Corinthians 9:25. You can't break the training regimen and win. That is true not only in athletics. It is true in everything. It is *especially* true in leadership.

Genuine success always comes at a high price. Every athlete knows this. That is why athletes regulate their sleep, what they eat, and how they exercise. It's not a part-time effort. For those who want to excel, it is a constant, nonstop responsibility.

Discipline has to become a passion. It isn't merely a question of doing whatever is mandatory and avoiding whatever is prohibited. It involves voluntary self-denial. An athlete has every right to eat a full eight-course dinner just before he runs the 100-yard dash. That's his privilege. But it's not smart. And if he doesn't sacrifice that right, he's not going to win.

Paul began 1 Corinthians 9 by making this very point. He had every right to be financially supported by those he ministered to (vv. 1–15). He had waived that right for their sake (vv. 12, 15), choosing to support himself as a tentmaker while he was living among them (Acts 18:3). "What is my reward then? That when I preach the gospel, I may present the gospel of Christ without charge, that I may not abuse my authority in the gospel" (1 Corinthians 9:18). "All things are lawful for me," he said, "but not all things are helpful; all things are lawful for me, but not all things edify" (10:23). He had voluntarily relinquished his apostolic rights for the sake of the Corinthians.

They, on the other hand, were so concerned about claiming their own rights that they were suing one another in secular courts (6:1–7). They were defiling the Lord's Supper by turning it into a contest over who got there first and who could get the most (11:21). They were so busy grasping at their rights, they were losing the prize. They were destroying their testimony and fragmenting the fellowship of the church. Virtually every problem in that church reflected a lack of discipline—an inability to control themselves and an unwillingness to forgo their own rights.

They desperately needed to follow Paul's example and show a little self-control. After all, if athletes can discipline themselves for the sake of a perishable prize, Christians certainly ought to be willing to do the same "for an imperishable crown" (9:25).

Why is discipline important? Discipline teaches us to operate by principle rather than desire. Saying no to our impulses (even the ones that are not inherently sinful) puts us in control of our appetites rather than vice versa. It deposes our lust and permits truth, virtue, and integrity to rule our minds instead.

We belong to an undisciplined society. The world we live in has enthroned the notion of personal rights and made restraint seem evil. But even in such a culture, those who rise to leadership will usually be the ones who practice a measure of self-control.

How can leaders develop self-discipline in an undisciplined world? With the hectic pace of modern life and the layers of complexity that have been added to life by so many modern "conveniences," is it possible to discipline oneself as a leader?

I'm convinced that it is, and I have found several practical suggestions to be personally helpful to develop self-discipline. When I'm asked to speak to leaders about leadership and self-discipline, I often give this list:

Get Organized

Start where you are. Clean your room. Put your desk in order. Put away things that are out of place, and throw away things that are useless. Make everything in your environment neat.

Make a list of priorities and put them in order. Then schedule your time so that everything gets done. Schedule the hardest and most undesirable tasks first, so that you can do them when you have the most energy. Break complex tasks into smaller steps, and schedule each phase of the process.

Personal organizers are very helpful, whether you prefer the high-tech style of computer-based personal information managers or the low-tech variety of a simple notebook or calendar. Use whatever suits your preference (even if it's just random scraps of paper), but keep it in one location and follow your plan.

If you don't have control of your time, you won't have control of any aspect of your life. And if you don't operate deliberately, on the schedule you have planned for yourself, your life will be ruled by crises and problem people. You cannot be an effective leader if you are always at the mercy of things out of your own control.

Use Time Wisely

Having made a plan for how you will use your time, follow it. Don't procrastinate. Work hard. Don't waste time. Stay busy. Be punctual. (Being late for appointments is a thoughtless waste of *other* people's time as well as your own.) Don't allow unnecessary interruptions or diversions to deflect you from your real priorities.

It is the epitome of foolishness to waste time. Paul wrote, "See then that you walk circumspectly, not as fools but as wise, redeeming the time, because the days are evil" (Ephesians 5:15–16). I have never met anyone who could habitually waste time and yet remain organized.

Of course, you need leisure time too. Jesus Himself recognized that rest is essential (Mark 6:31). But be organized and disciplined in that part of your life as well.

Find Ways to Be Edified Rather Than Merely Entertained

When you have time for rest and relaxation, do things that feed your soul rather than your carnal appetites. Listen to tapes of good preaching. Find music that uplifts and ennobles, rather than filling your mind with vanity and foolishness. Read a good book. Develop a hobby that has real value. Have an edifying conversation with someone you love.

This is a key component of true godliness: Give your private life to God. Devote yourself *especially* in your leisure time to the task of cultivating humility, repentance, holiness, and the fear of God.

Pay Attention to Small Things

If you're going to stay disciplined, you need to develop a habit of putting things where they belong. When you see a picture frame that is crooked, straighten it. When you see a weed, pull it. When you see something out of place, no matter how insignificant it may seem, put it away.

Small things are often important. Jesus told a parable in which the master commended a servant who was "faithful in a very little" (Luke 19:17). A lack of discipline in small matters often causes failure in the big things too. As the familiar nursery rhyme reminds us, whole kingdoms have been lost for the want of a horseshoe nail. Conversely, in my experience, those who are faithful in small things are the same people who are disciplined in more important matters too.

Accept Extra Responsibility

When you see something that needs to be done, volunteer. Meet others' needs whenever you can. Show yourself to be an industrious leader. Look for ways to use your gifts and resources for the good of others. This will help you focus your energies. It will also help you cultivate a servant's heart.

You have probably heard the old adage "If you want something done, ask someone who is busy." That's because hardworking people are the ones who get things done. Lethargy breeds a disorganized and undisciplined life, and learning to embrace extra responsibility is a good cure for lethargy.

Once You Start Something, Finish It

If you have a habit of starting projects you never finish, that is a sure sign of an undisciplined life. This goes back to the issue of planning. Good organization includes counting the cost. Jesus said it is a reproach to start something and not be able to finish (Luke 14:28–32). Why multiply projects when you haven't finished what you started before? Such a habit will quickly undermine people's confidence in you as a leader.

Keep Your Commitments

In a similar vein, don't say you'll do something you cannot do, and don't make a promise you don't intend to fulfill. Jesus said, "Let your 'Yes' be 'Yes,' and your 'No,' 'No'" (Matthew 5:37).

In other words, your word is your vow. And Scripture says, "When you make a vow to the LORD your God, you shall not delay to pay it; for the LORD your God will surely require it of you, and it would be sin to you. But if you abstain from vowing, it shall not be sin to you. That which has gone from your lips you shall keep and perform, for you voluntarily vowed to the LORD your God what you have promised with your mouth" (Deuteronomy 23:21–23).

A person who doesn't even keep his own commitments is invariably undisciplined in the rest of life.

Tell Yourself No from Time to Time

Gain control of your own appetites by denying yourself pleasures you may be entitled to. Skip dessert. Take a walk instead of taking a nap. Do something for your spouse rather than treating yourself.

That sort of self-denial is precisely what Paul was describing in 1 Corinthians 9:27: "I discipline my body and bring it into subjection." He used a Greek expression that literally means "to strike under the eye." In figurative terms, he was saying he made his own body a punching bag in order to cultivate discipline.

Notice how Paul painted this picture of self-discipline in vivid athletic terms. He wrote, "Therefore I run thus: not with uncertainty" (v. 26). He knew where the goal was. He knew where the boundaries of the track were. So he ran toward the prize with absolute determination. A runner with no goal and no boundaries will run aimlessly and lethargically. The Christian leader must keep the goal in view and run with persistence and with all his energy.

This, by the way, is another integral principle of leadership. It is a perfect partner to the principle of discipline: *A leader is energetic.*

I have never known an effective leader who was lazy or idle. Leaders must be industrious and diligent. This goes hand in hand with many of the principles we have highlighted so far. It is a necessary prerequisite to the

initiative, the enthusiasm, the decisiveness, and the resilience required in leadership.

The leader, like any good

> **Leadership Principle #24**
> **A LEADER IS ENERGETIC.**

athlete, cannot walk off the track midrace. He presses on toward the goal. In fact, as every athlete knows, we frequently must press on through pain, despite weariness, regardless of injury, against all opposition, and amid all kinds of trials. While it sometimes seems to drain every ounce of energy from the human reservoir, the success of the effort replenishes the spirit. The good leader, like the good athlete, sometimes has to reach deep within and find a way to persevere when perseverance seems impossible.

Paul knew exactly where he could draw such energy: "I can do all things through Christ who strengthens me" (Philippians 4:13). That's why he could say, "I know how to be abased, and I know how to abound. Everywhere and in all things I have learned both to be full and to be hungry, both to abound and to suffer need" (v. 12). He had disciplined himself to run, and to persevere through all difficulties, in such a way that he could achieve the prize.

Here Paul added another metaphor midverse. He was not only a runner; he was a boxer as well: "Therefore I run thus: not with uncertainty. Thus I fight: not as one who beats the air" (1 Corinthians 9:26). Notice he was not shadowboxing, and he was not sparring. He was in a serious fight. *While* he was running, he was also fighting. He had an opponent he had to keep punching out, because the opponent would otherwise get him off track.

This opponent, remember, was his own flesh—meaning the sinful tendencies that are so often associated with bodily appetites and carnal lusts. Now we know why he treated his own body like a punching bag. Otherwise, his own flesh would cause him to lose the race. He was running to win and boxing to keep from losing. In positive terms, he was cultivating the discipline of mental toughness to keep his eyes on the prize and his feet moving the right direction. In negative terms, he was cultivating the discipline of self-control in order to keep his own flesh from costing him the race.

Every athlete knows what this struggle is like. Every good athlete must keep his body under control. He can't be overweight, and he can't be unhealthy. He nourishes his body, exercises it to stay fit, and works it to build muscle. He stays in control of his body.

Most people, by contrast, are controlled by their bodies. Their bodies tell their minds what to do. "Feed me more. Don't overwork me. Give me pleasure. Give me rest." That is why the sin principle is called "the flesh" throughout the Pauline epistles. It is not that the body itself is inherently evil. But evil desires are often associated with the body. So Paul said we need to "put to death the deeds of the body" (Romans 8:13) and "[crucify] the flesh with its passions and desires" (Galatians 5:24).

The athlete has two things going for him: First, he knows how to subdue the body; and second, he has the mental toughness to keep pursuing his goal. Paul was saying that what makes a great athlete is the same discipline necessary for an effective leader.

But, he said, it is a perpetual discipline. If you slack off or give up before reaching the finish line, everything will be lost. That is why we must press on (Philippians 3:13–14) and run with endurance (Hebrews 12:1).

FINISHING THE RACE

For Paul, the passion to *finish* the race well was never far from the forefront of his thoughts. He told the Ephesian elders, "Chains and tribulations await me. But none of these things move me; nor do I count my life dear to myself, so that I may finish my race with joy" (Acts 20:23–24). When he wrote to the churches in Galatia, he rebuked them with these words: "You were running well; who hindered you from obeying the truth?" (Galatians 5:7 NASB). He also recounted for them how he had earnestly defended the gospel, "lest by any means I might run, or had run, in vain" (Galatians 2:2). He encouraged the Philippians to hold fast the Word of life, "so that I may rejoice in the day of Christ that I have not run in vain or labored in vain" (Philippians 2:16). He reminded Timothy that "if anyone competes in athletics, he is not crowned unless he competes according to the rules" (2 Timothy 2:5).

And here in 1 Corinthians 9, Paul explained that this was the very thing that motivated his careful, relentless self-discipline: "lest, when I have preached to others, I myself should become disqualified" (v. 27). That's true for any leader, not just preachers. The ultimate irony is the leader who disqualifies himself after having sought to influence others.

Paul drew this metaphor of disqualification straight from the Isthmian games. When the games began, a herald would enter the stadium with great pageantry. A trumpet was blown to call everyone to attention. Then the herald stood on a platform. He would announce the contest, read the names of all the contestants, and proclaim the rules. Of course, the rules were absolute and binding. Any infraction meant immediate disqualification.

Paul said he did not want to be the guy who proclaimed the rules but then disqualified *himself* by violating them.

There is no shortage of Christian leaders who have done precisely that. They seem to start well, and some even show signs of excellence for a time. But they don't finish well. They let their own flesh get in the way, and they are disqualified, even after they have preached to others. Some bail out because they prefer a life of ease to the trials of leadership. Others are set on the bench by divine Providence. More than a few are publicly disgraced after embarrassing the cause of Christ in reprehensible ways. They are nearly always disqualified because of their own lack of discipline.

Paul did not want that to happen to him. As a matter of fact, the yearning to finish well became the driving obsession of his life. He wanted to win the race for the glory and honor of Christ.

And he *did* finish well. He lived a triumphant life despite all his many trials. By most accounts, he was beheaded by the order of Nero on the Ostian Road near Rome. Paul knew his martyrdom was imminent, and shortly before he died, he wrote this classic valediction to his disciple Timothy:

> I am already being poured out as a drink offering, and the time of my departure is at hand. I have fought the good fight, I have finished the race, I have kept the faith. Finally, there is laid up for me the crown of righteousness, which the Lord, the righteous Judge, will give to me on that Day, and not to me only but also to all who have loved His appearing. (2 Timothy 4:6–8)

May that be our legacy too.

Chapter Eleven

———

WHO IS FIT TO LEAD?

I f we are to be faithful to the New Testament, we must acknowledge
that the Lord has established leaders in His church—pastors and
elders. They are the examples of spiritual leadership for all the
people, and if they are not exemplary leaders, something is seriously wrong.

The qualifications for elders and church leaders are not *just* for them.
These qualities are especially mandated for them because they set the pattern for all. "Like people, like priest" (Hosea 4:9). What the pastor and
elders are to be is the model for all Christians. And the principles that are
true of leaders in the church are also good principles for every Christian
in any position of leadership to apply.

So we have to look at what God requires of these model leaders in
order to know what is ultimately required of every leader.

We began chapter 1 of this book by observing that modern society is
suffering from a severe shortage of true leaders. The problem is closely
related to the dramatic moral decline that has been systematically eating
away at the foundations of our culture since (at least) the 1960s. Western
society no longer values *character*—integrity, decency, honor, loyalty,
truthfulness, purity, and other virtues. A look at the typical programming
on prime-time television instantly shows what the world thinks of such

qualities. They have been deposed. In their place, modern society has ensconced new and different values: selfishness, rebellion, rudeness, profane speech, irreverence, licentiousness, intemperance, and almost every kind of decadence. No wonder integrity is so hard to find.

Sadly, in this instance, what is true in the world is also true in the church. This is no secret. I was recently looking at a catalog from a Christian book retailer and noticed how many titles have been published over the past decade dealing with the integrity crisis in Christian leadership. The front cover of the catalog featured a half page of books on the subject. It is clear that there's a general feeling among Christians that failure is epidemic among their leaders.

Some segments of the visible church seem to have given up trying to find men of integrity to lead them. I recently read an article in the secular newspaper about a well-known pastor who resigned under pressure when his moral and financial improprieties became front-page news in his community. Four hundred people from his church left and started a new congregation so they could call him to be their pastor again. They said they loved the fact that he was so "human." One woman said she felt the scandal had equipped him to be a better pastor.

That is not a unique situation. A few years ago, another prominent pastor who left his church after a sordid sex scandal was immediately hired by one of the largest churches in the country to be part of their teaching staff. Within two weeks after the scandal made national news, he was back to preaching in the pulpit of a megachurch.

Worldly standards are gradually creeping into the church. The prevailing mood in the Christian community today is that no one is ever really disqualified from Christian leadership, but the disgraced leader who is willing to make a public show of remorse *ought* to be restored to a position of prominence as soon as possible. This means that in some circles, sexual immorality and marital infidelity are no longer deemed disqualifying sins for a pastor. I know of men who have dragged their churches through the grossest kinds of public scandal without missing a single week in the pulpit. Others take a little time off for "rehab" and "counseling," but then resume the leadership role. Sadly, this has become quite commonplace, because many in the church have responded to the leadership crisis by lowering expectations of their leaders.

How far we have come from the New Testament standard! Notice that in every list of qualifications the apostle Paul gave for church leaders, the first and most indispensable qualification for men in leadership was that they be "blameless" (1 Timothy 3:2, 10; Titus 1:6–7). Paul employed a Greek word that means "above reproach"—inculpable, unblemished, irreprehensible. Literally, it means "not subject to accusation." The term does not speak of sinlessness, of course, or no one would qualify (1 John 1:8). It does not disqualify people from leadership on the basis of sins they committed before conversion, or Paul himself would have been disqualified (1 Timothy 1:12–16). But it describes a person whose Christian testimony is free from the taint of scandal—someone who is upright, sound in character, and without any serious moral blemish. Simply put, it means leaders must have a reputation for unimpeachable integrity.

The early church held leaders to the highest moral and ethical standards. Nowhere is that more clear in Scripture than Acts 6, where Luke recorded how the first leaders were marked out and chosen by their fellow believers to assist the work of the apostles.

Of course, Christ Himself had already chosen and appointed the apostles (John 15:16). But remember that at Pentecost alone, three thousand people were added to the church (Acts 2:41). Another five thousand men (and presumably many more from their families) were added in Acts 4:4. Since we know that many were being added to the church daily, it appears the church in Jerusalem quickly grew to include at least ten thousand believers (and very likely more than twice that). Obviously, the time soon came when the responsibilities of leadership in the church were more than twelve apostles could handle.

Someone once said that Christians become very unchristian when they get organized. Sometimes that seems true. But Acts 6 reveals how things *ought* to be in the church.

Obviously, the early church was having a major impact on the Jewish community in Jerusalem. Multitudes were coming to faith in Jesus Christ. An amazing spirit of love and harmony existed among the Christians. Because so many in first-century Jerusalem were dispossessed and transient people, the community of believers "had all things in common, and sold their possessions and goods, and divided them among all, as anyone had need. So continuing daily with one accord in the temple, and breaking bread from house to house, they ate their food with gladness and simplicity of heart" (Acts 2:44–46).

The first hint of any controversy in the church comes in Acts 6:1, where Luke wrote, "Now in those days, when the number of the disciples was multiplying, there arose a complaint against the Hebrews by the Hellenists, because their widows were neglected in the daily distribution."

There were two groups of people in the early church. Since the church began in Jerusalem, practically all the early believers were Jewish. But some were *Hebrews,* and some were *Hellenists.* The Hebrews spoke Aramaic, a derivative of Hebrew. Most of them were native-born Judeans. The Hellenists were Jews who had adopted the Greek language and Greek lifestyle. Most of them were from Asia Minor, North Africa, and diverse places throughout the Roman Empire. But they remained loyal to the Jewish religion and returned en masse to Jerusalem every year for Passover season and Pentecost.

Many who were converted under Peter's preaching at Pentecost were therefore Hellenists. Many of them apparently remained in Jerusalem to become part of the Christian community. One of the main practical reasons the early church became such a caring and sharing body was the necessity of meeting the collective needs of this massive immigrant community.

Obviously, with so many believers from two major strains of culture, people would tend to associate with their own language group. Moreover, the Hebrews had been brought up to regard Hellenistic Jews with a degree of suspicion, because they felt they had been polluted by alien culture. The apostle Paul said that in his preconversion life, one of the things he took pride in was that he was "a Hebrew of the Hebrews" (Philippians

3:5)—not a Hellenistic Jew. Although he had been born in Tarsus, in Cilicia (a Gentile nation), he had been brought up in Jerusalem, at the feet of Gamaliel, a strict Pharisee and Hebrew rabbi. The Hebrews tended to think the Hellenists were not true Jews, because they had not remained loyal to the land and the traditions of Israel. So in that cultural friction lay the makings of a potentially serious conflict.

"The daily distribution" refers to the apostles' practice of dispensing food, money, and other resources to those in need (Acts 4:35), especially widows. The Grecian Jews were no doubt in the minority, and Luke said some of them began to feel the needs of the widows in their group were being neglected.

Obviously, a complaint like that can easily become a wedge that splits the church. As any church leader will testify, no matter how petty such murmuring may appear, it always has the potential for great mischief. In this case, it may have been true that some of the Grecian widows were being overlooked. Obviously, it wasn't intentional, but the situation needed to be corrected.

So the apostles responded quickly. Luke described what happened:

> The twelve summoned the multitude of the disciples and said, "It is not desirable that we should leave the word of God and serve tables. Therefore, brethren, seek out from among you seven men of good reputation, full of the Holy Spirit and wisdom, whom we may appoint over this business; but we will give ourselves continually to prayer and to the ministry of the word." And the saying pleased the whole multitude. And they chose Stephen, a man full of faith and the Holy Spirit, and Philip, Prochorus, Nicanor, Timon, Parmenas, and Nicolas, a proselyte from Antioch, whom they set before the apostles; and when they had prayed, they laid hands on them. Then the word of God spread, and the number of the disciples multiplied greatly in Jerusalem, and a great many of the priests were obedient to the faith. (Acts 6:2–7)

The church had become too big for twelve leaders. Such a large community desperately needed more oversight and more organization. So the apostles proposed a plan for the people themselves to appoint godly men with outstanding reputations to come alongside and "serve tables," meaning that these men would now oversee the distribution of food and funds to those in need.

Seven men were to be singled out to serve in a subordinate leadership role. They were appointed to serve, which is normally the role of a deacon, and for that reason, commentators sometimes refer to them as the first deacons. But notice that the text does not call them deacons. At least two of them, Stephen and Philip, were also preachers, which is a role more associated with elders than with deacons (1 Timothy 3:2; Titus 1:9). Of course, they're not called elders, either. This was so early in the formulation of the church that those offices did not even exist yet. When the apostle Paul listed the qualifications for deacons and elders in 1 Timothy 3, the only significant difference between the two offices was that elders must be gifted to teach. Elders are given the teaching authority in the church, and deacons serve under them in a support role, much the way these seven men in Acts 6 were appointed to do under the apostles.

In many churches, the deaconate is somewhat of a training ground for elders. It is not uncommon in the church I pastor for deacons to become elders as they develop their skill in teaching and their ability to handle the Word. That process began here in Acts 6. As these seven men proved themselves faithful in serving, at least some of them, like Philip and Stephen, also developed skill as teachers. No doubt some of them later stepped into even greater roles of leadership as the apostles were martyred or moved on to take the gospel message to the remotest parts of the earth. As they proved their faithfulness and assumed greater leadership roles, new servant leaders would have been appointed to serve alongside them. Eventually, the teaching role was designated as the office of an elder, and the servant role was assigned to officers called deacons.

So what we see in Acts 6 are the rudimentary beginnings of church organization. The separate offices of elders and deacons are foreshadowed in this event, but they were not yet clearly defined.

From this passage, however, we learn much about how the church is to be organized and what kind of leaders ought to have oversight. At least three principles emerge that continue to set the standard for all leaders in the church. Notice the *plurality* of leadership that was prescribed; the *priority* that was recognized as leadership's first duty; and the standard of *purity* that was demanded of those who were appointed. We will examine each of these closely, because they establish principles that apply to spiritual leaders of all kinds.

PLURALITY

The clear New Testament pattern for church government is a plurality of God-ordained men who lead the people of God together. The church is not to be led by dictators, autocrats, or solitary rulers. From the beginning, oversight was shared by twelve apostles, and we see here that when they appointed subordinate leaders, those men also functioned as a team.

When Paul and Barnabas founded churches in Asia Minor, Luke said they "appointed elders in every church" (Acts 14:23). Paul likewise instructed Titus to "appoint elders in every city as I commanded you" (Titus 1:5). At the end of Paul's third missionary journey, "he sent to Ephesus and called for the elders of the church" (Acts 20:17). In Jerusalem, Paul met with "James, and all the elders" (Acts 21:18). Virtually every time elders are spoken of in Scripture in connection with a church, the noun is plural, clearly indicating that the standard practice in the New Testament was for multiple elders to oversee each church.

Every ministry described in the New Testament was a team effort. Jesus called twelve disciples. After Judas's betrayal and suicide, Matthias was chosen to take his place (Acts 1:16–26). Those twelve as apostles obviously shared oversight in the founding and early ministry of the Jerusalem church. When they began to take the gospel to "all Judea and

Samaria, and to the end of the earth" (Acts 1:8), they did so in teams (Acts 15:22–27; Galatians 2:9).

Peter and John together dominate the first twelve chapters of Acts. The focus shifts to Paul and Barnabas in Acts 13. Then Barnabas went with Mark, and Paul went with Silas at the end of Acts 15. Timothy joined Paul and Silas in Acts 16. When Paul returned to Antioch in Acts 18, he took Aquila and Priscilla along. As we have seen, Paul even took Luke and Aristarchus with him on his journey to Rome, although he was a prisoner of the Roman government at the time. A comprehensive list of all of Paul's various companions and fellow ministers would fill a page or more.

In other words, ministry as depicted in the New Testament was never a one-man show. That does not preclude the role of a dominant leader on each team. Within the framework of plurality, there will invariably be those who have more influence. The diversity of our gifts (1 Corinthians 12:4) means all people are differently equipped. Therefore a plurality of leaders does not necessitate an absolute equality in every function. In even the most godly group of leaders, some will naturally be more influential than others. Some will have teaching gifts that outshine the rest. Others will be more gifted as administrators. Each can fulfill a different role, and there is no need to try to enforce absolute equality of function.

The Twelve, for example, are always listed in similar order in Scripture (Matthew 10:2–4; Mark 3:16–19; Luke 6:14–16; Acts 1:13). They seem to divide naturally into four groups. The first four names listed are always Peter, James, John, and Andrew. Peter's name always heads the list, and the other three are listed in varying order. Those four dominate the gospel narratives, and three of them are often seen with Christ apart from the other nine (Matthew 17:1; Mark 5:37; 13:3; 14:33).

The second group includes Philip, Bartholomew, Thomas, and Matthew. Philip's name always heads that list, but the other three are ordered differently in different places. The third group consists of James, Thaddaeus (or Lebbaeus, also known as Judas, son of James), Simon, and Judas Iscariot. James's name always heads that list.

So each group seems to have had its unofficial leader. Peter was usually the leader and spokesman for all twelve. Their office and their privileges were equal, but their influence and importance varied according to their gifts and personalities.

Nothing suggests that Peter had a higher office than the others. He certainly is never portrayed as a pope in the Bible. In Acts 15:19, for example, it was James ("the Lord's brother," according to Galatians 1:19, not one of the Twelve) who announced the Jerusalem Council's decision, even though Peter was present and testified. And in Antioch, the apostle Paul withstood Peter "to his face, because he was to be blamed" when he compromised with the Judaizers (Galatians 2:11). Peter clearly wielded no more authority and held no higher office than the other twelve, although he plainly was the strongest leader in the group. As noted, Peter and John together dominate the early chapters of Acts. But Peter was always the spokesman and preacher. John, of course, had equal authority, and (partly because he lived longer) he wrote more of the New Testament than Peter, including the gospel that bears his name, three epistles, and Revelation. But when John and Peter were together, Peter always did the speaking. Likewise, although Barnabas obviously had remarkable teaching gifts, Paul was always the dominant member of that duo.

It should be apparent, then, that the biblical concept of team leadership does not demand an artificial or absolute equality. There's nothing wrong, in other words, with a church's appointing a senior pastor, or a pastor-teacher. Those who claim otherwise have misunderstood the biblical approach to plural leadership.

Still, the undeniable biblical pattern is for multiple elders, team leadership, and shared responsibility—never one-man rule. And leadership by a plurality of godly men has several strong advantages. Proverbs 11:14 says, "Where there is no counsel, the people fall; but in the multitude of counselors there is safety." The sharing of the leadership burden also increases accountability and helps ensure that the decisions of leadership are not self-willed or self-serving.

One-man leadership and autocratic rule are the hallmarks of cults and false religions. Although well-suited for men like Diotrephes, who loved to have the preeminence (3 John 9), it is not the proper model for a biblical church.

It is fitting, therefore, that when the apostles first appointed subordinate leaders in the Jerusalem church, they appointed a team of seven.

PRIORITY

The burden of personal need in the Jerusalem church had grown to such proportions that the Twelve, in order to serve everyone, had to "leave the word of God" (Acts 6:2). In other words, they had out of sheer pragmatic necessity been forced to curtail the time they spent studying and proclaiming the Scriptures. Even so, they still weren't able to manage the distribution process well enough to keep everyone happy. They knew they needed to delegate the task to others who could oversee that task and better organize the process. They understood something with which every wise leader has to come to grips, sooner rather than later: you simply cannot do everything yourself. *A leader knows how to delegate.*

It is simply not wise leadership to try to manage everything with hands-on oversight. Leaders who take that approach invariably frustrate their people by micromanaging, and they sabotage their own effectiveness by getting bogged down in details. A few things demand your hands-on attention, but good leadership demands that you delegate the rest. There is no other way to get all the work done and keep your attention on your priorities.

Moses learned the art of delegation from his father-in-law. Exodus 18:14 says, "When Moses' father-in-law saw all that he did for the people, he said, 'What is this thing that you are doing for the people? Why do you alone sit, and all the people stand before you from morning until evening?'"

Moses explained that people came to him to settle all their disputes. "When they have a difficulty, they come to me, and I judge between one and another; and I make known the statutes of God and His laws" (v. 16).

So Moses' father-in-law said to him, "The thing that you do is not good. Both you and these people who are with you will surely wear yourselves out. For this thing is too much for you; you are not able to perform it by yourself. Listen now to my voice; I will give you counsel, and God will be with you: Stand before God for the people, so that you may bring the difficulties to God. And you shall teach them the statutes and the laws, and show them the way in which they must walk and the work they must do. Moreover you shall select from all the people able men, such as fear God, men of truth, hating covetousness; and place such over them to be rulers

---

Leadership Principle #25

A LEADER KNOWS HOW TO DELEGATE.

---

of thousands, rulers of hundreds, rulers of fifties, and rulers of tens. And let them judge the people at all times. Then it will be that every great matter they shall bring to you, but every small matter they themselves shall judge. So it will be easier for you, for they will bear the burden with you. If you do this thing, and God so commands you, then you will be able to endure, and all this people will also go to their place in peace."

So Moses heeded the voice of his father-in-law and did all that he had said. And Moses chose able men out of all Israel, and made them heads over the people: rulers of thousands, rulers of hundreds, rulers of fifties, and rulers of tens. So they judged the people at all times; the hard cases they brought to Moses, but they judged every small case themselves (vv. 17–26).

It was a wise strategy, and God blessed it.

When I first came to Grace Community Church, I gathered a group of men who would meet with me on Saturday mornings. We studied principles of church leadership together, and I began delegating tasks to them. As they proved themselves faithful and able, several of them became lay elders in our church. Others saw their ministries develop to the point that we brought them on staff full-time. In that way, for the first decade or more of my ministry here, we developed virtually the entire staff and leadership of our church from within the church itself. That is how ministry is supposed to work: Pastors "[equip] the saints for the work of ministry" (Ephesians 4:12). Paul encouraged Timothy to raise up leaders that way: "The things that you have heard from me among many witnesses, commit these to faithful men who will be able to teach others also" (2 Timothy 2:2). This is one of the chief values of delegation: It helps equip others to lead. The leader who follows that plan will reproduce more leaders.

When you delegate duties to others, remember to delegate only what you are willing to let go of. And then give the people you delegate the freedom to fail. Don't take back what you have delegated. But teach them when they fail that they need to be quick to learn to make a good second decision. As they learn to do things with excellence, you can delegate more, and do it with confidence.

How do you decide what you are willing to delegate to others? You need to have a clear understanding of your priorities. Your own priorities, not someone else's emergencies, should determine what you do and what you delegate to others. That is what happened in the Jerusalem church.

Luke wonderfully outlined the hierarchy of priorities embraced by the leaders of the early church. The Twelve said, "It is not desirable that we should leave the word of God and serve tables . . . but we will give ourselves continually to prayer and to the ministry of the word" (Acts 6:2–4). Notice the three main activities that dominated their energies—prayer, the ministry of the Word of God, and servant ministry—in that order.

Those three activities consumed the apostles' time and efforts, and they are a pattern for church leaders even today. They perfectly outline the main business of the church, and therefore set the agenda for all church leaders. The order is clear. Servant ministry, while crucial, is not to eclipse prayer and the ministry of the Word.

That simple fact seems lost on many these days. Ask the typical pulpit committee what they are looking for in a pastor, and you can practically guarantee that prayer will not be at the top of the list. Even preaching isn't always given a very high priority. Submit a list of candidates to the typical church, and they will probably choose the candidate who is the most affable, gregarious, and sociable—someone who is willing to do lots of visitation and host lots of church socials, rather than a man who devotes himself to prayer and study. Others will look for a man with administrative or entrepreneurial talents, because they think of the church as a secular enterprise. The apostolic priorities have thus been eclipsed by other business in too many churches.

Look at these priorities individually:

Prayer

We're not inclined to think of prayer as work. We tend to think of prayer as inactivity. But it is not. Good praying is hard work, and prayer is the first and most important work of all ministry. All other activities of ministry are utterly futile if not bathed in prayer.

Prayer itself is, after all, an implicit recognition of the sovereignty of God. We know that we cannot change people's hearts, so we pray for God to do it. We know that it is the Lord who adds to His church, so we pray to Him as Lord of the harvest. We know that "unless the LORD builds the house, they labor in vain who build it; unless the LORD guards the city, the watchman stays awake in vain" (Psalm 127:1).

We can plant, and we can water, but no aspect of ministry can ultimately be fruitful unless God Himself gives the increase (cf. 1 Corinthians 3:6–7). Our efforts can never bear fruit unless they are blessed by God. Jesus said, "Without Me you can do nothing" (John 15:5). Since that is true, isn't it obvious that everything we do ought to be bathed in prayer?

That is why our first and most essential priority is prayer. Paul wrote, "Therefore I exhort *first of all* that supplications, prayers, intercessions, and giving of thanks be made" (1 Timothy 2:1, emphasis added). We are to "pray without ceasing" (1 Thessalonians 5:17). We're taught by Scripture to pray earnestly, persistently, frequently, and soberly. Peter said, "The end of all things is at hand; therefore be serious and watchful in your prayers" (1 Peter 4:7). This is the first priority in all our work.

Good praying *is* hard labor—make no mistake about it. It is hard to stay focused. It is no easy task to intercede for others. But the wise leader will not neglect this first order of business. Nothing, no matter how vital it may seem, is more urgent. And therefore we must not let anything else crowd prayer off our already-busy agendas.

My advice is to start each day with a specific time of prayer. Don't let interruptions or appointments distract you from your first business. Go to the Lord when your mind is fresh. Prayer is hard enough work without putting it off until your mind is fatigued. Don't squander your brightest hours doing less-important things.

But don't limit your praying to mornings. "[Pray] always with all prayer and supplication in the Spirit, being watchful to this end with all perseverance and supplication for all the saints" (Ephesians 6:18).

The Ministry of the Word

Paul told Timothy, "Preach the word! Be ready in season and out of season. Convince, rebuke, exhort, with all longsuffering and teaching" (2 Timothy 4:2). This duty, like prayer, is hard work. Devoting oneself to the ministry of the Word means spending time in study. It is a total commitment. "We will give ourselves *continually* to prayer and to the ministry of the word" (Acts 6:4, emphasis added).

That may occasionally require the faithful pastor to neglect what seems urgent in order to do what is really essential. That can be difficult, because the demands of ministry and leadership are so great. But we *must* keep this priority straight.

That is precisely why the apostles saw the need to appoint leaders in a support role. The apostles' time was being consumed by legitimate, urgent needs in the church. They were spending so much time serving tables that they were neglecting the more essential, higher priorities of prayer and the ministry of the Word. Something had to change.

Servant Ministry

Notice that the apostles did not regard the task of serving tables as something that was dispensable. They were not willing to leave the distribution of charity undone. And they were not suggesting that waiting tables was beneath them because they had achieved the rank of apostle. But there was too much work for them to do it all without neglecting their more important duties. And so they appointed men in a support role—men who could serve alongside them to meet all these needs.

This is the whole point of servant leadership. We are servants, leading and training other servants; thus, the ministry becomes a self-perpetuating school for servants. Jesus modeled that kind of discipleship during His earthly life, and He always maintained the perfect balance, never neglecting prayer or the ministry of the Word for the sake of meeting mundane needs, but never letting people's needs go unmet.

Following their Lord's own example, the apostles therefore delegated the oversight of the servant ministries to "seven men of good reputation, full of the Holy Spirit and wisdom" (Act 6:3).

PURITY

Notice that the men chosen to oversee that vital third priority were chosen for their character and reputation, not because of their social stature, their experience in the business world, their raw abilities, or any of the other criteria churches today often employ in selecting leaders. A lowly slave of unimpeachable character is more suitable for spiritual leadership than a business magnate whose integrity is questionable. A man is qualified for this role because of what he *is*, not merely because of what he *does*. The stress is always on character more than ability. Purity, not personality, is the key issue.

Why this high standard? Because whatever the leaders are, the people become. Spiritual leaders set the example for others to follow. As Hosea said, "Like people, like priest" (Hosea 4:9). Jesus said, "Everyone who is perfectly trained will be like his teacher" (Luke 6:40). People will not rise above the spiritual level of their leadership.

The new leaders therefore were to be men of "good reputation" (Acts 6:3). Paul said leaders in the church must have good reputations both inside the church and among unbelievers as well (1 Timothy 3:7).

The men chosen to assist the apostles in leadership also had to be "full of the Holy Spirit and wisdom" (Acts 6:3). That means they had to be *controlled* by the Holy Spirit (cf. Ephesians 5:18) and men of sober, righteous judgment.

The men who were chosen all had Greek names, suggesting that they were predominantly if not exclusively from the Hellenist community. Nicolas was "a proselyte from Antioch" (Acts 6:5)—a Gentile who had converted to Judaism before becoming a Christian. This was a loving expression of the early church's unity. In all likelihood, most in the Jerusalem church were Hebrews, and yet they acknowledged the godly leadership of their Hellenistic brethren. Thus a potential rift was healed, and the church got back to business with its priorities in order.

The seven men were set before the apostles, formally ordained, and put to work (v. 6). The apostles devoted themselves anew to prayer and the ministry of the Word. "Then the word of God spread, and the number of the disciples multiplied greatly in Jerusalem, and a great many of the priests were obedient to the faith" (v. 7).

The church's zeal seems to have been invigorated and its influence expanded by the efficiency of the new organization. After all, it gave the apostles new freedom to do what they were called to do. It unleashed the Word of God. No wonder growth increased exponentially. And the impact of the church's evangelistic ministry reached right into the temple. A revival broke out among the priests. As a result, many of the very men who had been the most bitter opponents of Christ during His earthly ministry were converted to the Christian faith.

All of this underscores the supreme importance of having the right kind of leaders. Mere talent could never have such a powerful influence. This wasn't about style or strategy or flowcharts. It was about choosing men of character to lead the people of God, so that the work of the ministry would get done in the right way, by the right people, devoted to the right priorities.

We have come back to our starting point. Leadership is all about *character*—honor,

> **Leadership Principle #26**
> **A LEADER IS CHRISTLIKE.**

decency, integrity, faithfulness, holiness, moral purity, and other qualities like these.

All these virtues may be combined and summed up in one final statement. This rounds out and perfectly summarizes every fundamental requirement of a true leader: *A leader is Christlike.*

The perfect model of true leadership, of course, is the Great Shepherd, Christ Himself. If that does not make you feel the least bit unworthy, you have missed the whole point. With Paul, we ought to say, "Who is sufficient for these things?" (2 Corinthians 2:16).

We already know the answer: "Our sufficiency is from God" (3:5).

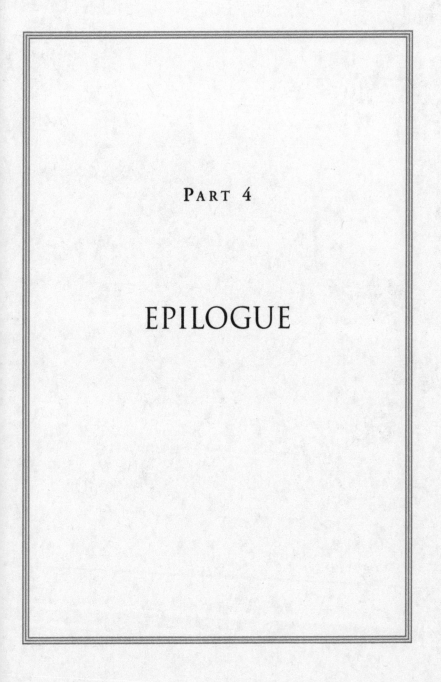

PART 4

EPILOGUE

Chapter Twelve

THE MEASURE OF
A LEADER'S SUCCESS

If we judged success by worldly standards, some might be inclined to assess Paul's leadership career as an abject failure and a bitter disappointment. In the closing days of his life, when Paul wrote 2 Timothy, Luke was virtually his only contact with the outside world (4:11). Paul was confined in a Roman dungeon, dreading the savage cold of coming winter (vv. 13, 21), and without any hope of deliverance from the death sentence that had been imposed on him. He suffered because of the sadistic contempt of his enemies. He was even abandoned or disavowed by some of his closest friends. He wrote, "This you know, that all those in Asia have turned away from me" (2 Timothy 1:15).

"Asia" refers to Asia Minor, where Paul had focused his missionary work. Ephesus, where Timothy pastored, was the capital of that region. So Paul wasn't telling Timothy anything Timothy didn't already know first-hand. In that time of fierce persecution, association with Paul had become so costly that all but a few of the apostle's own spiritual children had in effect disowned and abandoned him.

That's why people who see things superficially might think the end of

181

Paul's life was tragic. At first glance, it might even seem as if his enemies had finally defeated him.

A failure? Actually, the apostle Paul was not a failure as a leader by any measure. His influence continues worldwide even today. By contrast, Nero, the corrupt but powerful Roman emperor who ordered Paul's death, is one of history's most despised figures. This is yet another reminder that *influence* is the true test of a person's leadership, not power or position per se. In fact, a careful look at how Paul's life and ministry came to an end can teach us a lot about how to gauge the success or failure of a leader.

Paul's first long imprisonment and trial before Nero apparently ended in the apostle's release sometime before AD 64, because he wrote the epistles of 1 Timothy and Titus as a free man (1 Timothy 3:14–15; 4:13; Titus 3:12). But that liberty was short-lived. In July of the year 64, seven of Rome's fourteen districts burned. When the original fire was nearly extinguished, another fire, fanned by fierce winds, broke out in another district. Rumors circulated that Nero himself had ordered the burning of the city in order to make room for some ambitious building projects, including a golden palace for himself.

Trying desperately to deflect suspicion, Nero blamed Christians for starting the fires. That began the first of several major, aggressive campaigns by the Roman government to destroy the church. Christians in Rome were rounded up and executed in unspeakably cruel ways. Some were sewn into animal skins and ripped to death by dogs. Others were impaled on stakes, covered with pitch, and burned as human torches to light Nero's garden parties. Many were beheaded, fed to lions, or otherwise disposed of at Nero's command in equally ruthless ways.

During that persecution, Paul was again taken prisoner by the Roman authorities, brought to Rome, subjected to persecution and torment (2 Timothy 4:17), and finally executed as a traitor because of his relentless devotion to the lordship of Christ.

Throughout his first imprisonment at Rome, Paul had been kept under house arrest (Acts 28:16, 30). He was allowed freedom to preach and teach those who visited him (v. 23). He was under the constant guard of a Roman soldier but was treated with respect. The influence of his ministry had therefore reached right into the household of Caesar (Philippians 4:22).

Paul's second imprisonment, however, was markedly different. He was virtually cut off from all outside contact and kept chained in a dungeon (2 Timothy 1:16). He was probably held underground in the Mamertine Prison, adjacent to the Roman forum, in a small, dark, bare stone dungeon whose only entrance was a hole in the ceiling scarcely large enough for one person to pass through. The dungeon itself is not large; about half the size of a small one-car garage. Yet it was sometimes used to hold as many as forty prisoners. The discomfort, the dark, the stench, and the misery were almost unbearable.

That dungeon still exists, and I have been in it. The stifling, claustrophobic confines of that dark hole are eerie and depressing even today. It was there (or in a dungeon just like it) that Paul spent the final days of his life.

There is no reliable record of Paul's execution, but he obviously knew the end of his life was imminent when he wrote his second epistle to Timothy. Evidently he had already been tried, convicted, and condemned for preaching Christ, and perhaps the day of his execution was already scheduled. He wrote to Timothy, "I am already being poured out as a drink offering, and the time of my departure is at hand" (2 Timothy 4:6).

Naturally, there are notes of profound sadness in Paul's final epistle. But its dominant theme is triumph, not defeat. Paul wrote that last letter to Timothy to encourage the young pastor to be bold and courageous and to continue following the example he had learned from his apostolic mentor. Far from writing a concession of failure, Paul sounds a clarion note of victory: "I have fought the good fight, I have finished the race, I have kept the faith. Finally, there is laid up for me the crown of righteousness, which the

Lord, the righteous Judge, will give to me on that Day, and not to me only but also to all who have loved His appearing" (2 Timothy 4:7–8).

Facing his own imminent martyrdom, Paul had no fear, no despondency, and no desire to stay in this world. He longed to be with Christ and eagerly anticipated the reward He would receive in the next world. Therefore, as he reviewed the course of his life, he expressed no regret, no sense of unfulfillment, and no feeling of incompleteness. There was not the smallest duty left undone. He had finished the work the Lord gave him to do, just as in Acts 20:24 he had hoped and prayed he would do: "so that I may finish my race with joy."

Paul measured his own success as a leader, as an apostle, and as a Christian by a single criterion: He had "kept the faith"—meaning both that he had remained faithful to Christ and that he had kept the message of Christ's gospel intact, just as he had received it. He had proclaimed the Word of God faithfully and fearlessly. And now he was passing the baton to Timothy and to others, who would be "able to teach others also" (2 Timothy 2:2).

Therefore, Paul faced his own death with a triumphant spirit and with a deep sense of joy. He had seen the grace of God accomplish all that God designed in him and through him, and now he was ready to meet Christ face-to-face.

In the closing section of 2 Timothy, as Paul finished the last chapter of his final epistle—as he wrote what would literally stand as the concluding paragraph of his life—what filled the heart and mind of this great leader were the people he ministered to and worked alongside. He spoke of several individuals who had been part of his life. They were the most visible and immediate legacy of his leadership. Although he was left virtually friendless in prison, although he had been forsaken at his defense before a Roman tribunal, he was clearly *not* alone in life.

In fact, the true character of Paul's leadership is seen in this brief list of people he had poured his life into. They personified the team he built, the treachery he endured, the trials he suffered, and the triumph he ultimately obtained. This catalog of individuals is therefore instructive in assessing why Paul's leadership was not a failure. This is why his influence continues to be an example to millions of Christians even today.

THE TEAM HE BUILT

What we have in the closing paragraph of 2 Timothy is an abbreviated sample of the network of people whom Paul depended on in his ministry. Here we are reminded that none of us who would serve Christ can do so alone. We are not islands. Although leadership is sometimes a lonely calling, the true leader must never be isolated from people. Just as people need leaders, leaders need people. Leadership itself is by definition a process of team building. Moses needed Aaron and Hur to hold up his hands (Exodus 17:12). When David was an outcast, he gathered men who were distressed, in debt, and discontented, and he made an army of them (1 Samuel 22:2). Even Jesus' earthly ministry was devoted to training a few individuals, and at the hour of His soul's deepest agony, He asked three of them to watch with Him in prayer (Matthew 26:37–41).

The more we cultivate people to depend on, and the more we learn to delegate, the better we can lead. The more a leader invests his life in people, the more effective that person will be in the Lord's service.

The modern business world illustrates how vital networking is to success in leadership. The world of commerce depends on sophisticated networks of suppliers, customers, government agencies, stockholders, employees, and management. Scripture compares the church to a body to make this very point (1 Corinthians 12:14–27). The human body is perhaps the most graphic visual demonstration of networking as we live and move in an incredible network of organs, muscles, tissue, blood, and bones that all function in perfect harmony.

Paul had built a network of people around him. He had a large and effective team. He had many people on whom he depended, people to whom he delegated responsibility, and people in whom he trusted. Among them were some who were constantly faithful, some who proved unfaithful; some who remained friends no matter what, some who turned away from Paul in trials; some who became longtime partners, some who were short-term accomplices; some who were consistent, some who were inconsistent; some who were always ready to volunteer, and some who were never ready to volunteer. They were all a part of his life, and all were influenced in one way or another by his leadership.

As Paul faced the ax that would cut off his head and knew that his life was about to end, those people were on his mind. Remember, he wrote his two epistles to Timothy in order to pass the mantle of church leadership to his young protégé. And one vital step in that process required him to inform Timothy about what was going on with all the people on the team. In this farewell paragraph, he sounds like an old coach turning over the team to a young coach. The young coach needs to know where everyone plays so he can step in as the team leader with a minimum of trauma and difficulty. Paul wrote:

> Be diligent to come to me quickly; for Demas has forsaken me, having loved this present world, and has departed for Thessalonica—Crescens for Galatia, Titus for Dalmatia. Only Luke is with me. Get Mark and bring him with you, for he is useful to me for ministry. And Tychicus I have sent to Ephesus. Bring the cloak that I left with Carpus at Troas when you come—and the books, especially the parchments. Alexander the coppersmith did me much harm. May the Lord repay him according to his works. You also must beware of him, for he has greatly resisted our words. At my first defense no one stood with me, but all forsook me. May it not be charged against them.
>
> But the Lord stood with me and strengthened me, so that the message might be preached fully through me, and that all the Gentiles might hear. Also I was delivered out of the mouth of the lion. And the Lord will deliver me from every evil work and

THE MEASURE OF A LEADER'S SUCCESS   187

preserve me for His heavenly kingdom. To Him be glory forever
and ever. Amen!

Greet Prisca and Aquila, and the household of Onesiphorus.
Erastus stayed in Corinth, but Trophimus I have left in Miletus
sick. Do your utmost to come before winter. Eubulus greets you,
as well as Pudens, Linus, Claudia, and all the brethren. The Lord
Jesus Christ be with your spirit. Grace be with you. Amen.
(2 Timothy 4:9–22)

Some of the people Paul mentioned in that passage were close friends
whom he wanted with him in his last days, both for mutual comfort and
to assist him in the ministry that would carry on even after his death.
Those included Timothy, Luke, and Mark. Some were partners in ministry whom he mentioned simply to greet and share his love and his
concern because they, too, were lifelong friends. Those included Priscilla,
Aquila, and the family of Onesiphorus. Some whom he mentioned he had
already said good-bye to and sent to serve in strategic places to keep the
work strong. Those included Crescens, Titus, Tychicus, Erastus, and
Trophimus. Some whom he mentioned were sending their own greetings
to Timothy. Those were faithful believers living in Rome, including
Eubulus, Pudens, Linus, Claudia, and others. He also mentioned some
because of the intense grief they brought him. Those included Demas,
Alexander, and several anonymous deserters.

People, not programs, were on Paul's mind as he came to the end of
his life. People are the most vital and valuable resource any leader can cultivate. Paul had the happy privilege of living a life that fulfilled the words
of 1 Samuel 10:26, which says this about Saul: "Valiant men went with
him, whose hearts God had touched."

Paul had a band of men and women whose hearts God had touched
too. He wanted Timothy to know who they were, where they were, and
what they were doing as Timothy took over the reins of leadership. Notice
whom he mentioned, beginning with Timothy himself.

Timothy

Paul longed to see Timothy face-to-face one more time. In verse 9 he wrote, "Be diligent to come to me quickly." Paul regarded Timothy as "a true son in the faith" and "a beloved son" (1 Timothy 1:2; 2 Timothy 1:2). Timothy was in a sense a reproduction of the apostle, and that is why he was to be the heir of Paul's mantle of leadership.

In writing to the Corinthians about his tremendous concern for them, Paul had said to them in 1 Corinthians 4:17, "For this reason I have sent Timothy to you, who is my beloved and faithful son in the Lord, who will remind you of my ways in Christ, as I teach everywhere in every church." He regarded Timothy as a clone of himself, a carbon copy of his leadership. He trusted Timothy's teaching and knew the young pastor would teach people just what he himself had taught.

Timothy was unique in that regard. Paul likewise had written to the Philippians, "I trust in the Lord Jesus to send Timothy to you shortly, that I also may be encouraged when I know your state. For I have no one like-minded, who will sincerely care for your state" (Philippians 2:19–20). Timothy more than anyone else had the heart of Paul. He had the habits of Paul. He had the theology of Paul. He was Paul reproduced—the faithful son.

Therefore, as Paul sat in that cold, dark dungeon, he longed to see his dear friend and beloved son in the faith. He began 2 Timothy by writing, "I remember you in my prayers night and day, greatly desiring to see you, being mindful of your tears, that I may be filled with joy" (1:3–4). Although Paul's work was finished, there was much work yet to be done in the churches. No doubt Paul had much more to say to Timothy in person before Timothy took the mantle of leadership. He had things to say that could not be set down in a brief epistle. So he urged his faithful son to come.

He said, "Be *diligent* to come . . . *quickly.*" There's an urgency in the plea. Time was of the essence. Paul would be executed soon. Winter was approaching (v. 21), after which travel would be impossible because the seas would be too rough. There was much yet to say, and Paul wanted Timothy by his side as soon as possible.

Most great men owe their leadership skills to the influence of a mentor. They learn from someone whose heart they desire to emulate. For Timothy it was Paul. And Timothy was Paul's number one son in the faith. Mutually they had bound their lives together by God's wonderful grace and had found strength in one another.

One of the richest joys we will ever know as a leader in ministry occurs when God gives us the privilege of raising up Timothys, those who not only desire to hear what we say but who also emulate our example. As a young man, Timothy had struggled with fear and timidity, but he turned out to be a faithful son in every way. Like Paul, he was even imprisoned for his faithfulness (Hebrews 13:23). He became everything Paul had hoped.

Every true leader can thank God when by His grace He gives us spiritual children who are like Timothy, reproductions of ourselves. In the best cases, they become even better than we are, more devoted than we are, more godly than we are. But they catch the vision of our hearts and make the commitment to live to the glory of God and carry on the work to which we have devoted our lives.

Timothy contrasted starkly with Demas, whom we'll discuss shortly. Demas, as we shall see, proved to be as unfaithful as Timothy was faithful. Virtually everyone who is in leadership for any amount of time will eventually suffer the disappointment of a Demas. But faithful souls like Timothy are the true backbone of the team.

Skipping Demas for the moment, notice the next two names Paul mentions: "Crescens has gone to Galatia, Titus to Dalmatia" (2 Timothy 4:10 NASB).

Crescens

Nothing is known about Crescens except for this mention of his name. Don't assume because he is named in the same verse as Demas that he falls into the same category of unfaithfulness. If that were the case, Titus wouldn't also be grouped with them. We know that Titus, like Timothy, was regarded by Paul as "a true son in our common faith" (Titus 1:4). Therefore, in this context, Paul was simply reporting how his friends had been dispersed into various regions of Asia Minor. He expressly stated that Demas had abandoned him. He said no such thing about Crescens or Titus.

Crescens had gone to Galatia—probably at the behest of Paul himself—to care for the troubled church there. Evidently Crescens was a capable and trustworthy man, or Paul would never have sent him to Galatia. Galatia was a region where Paul had labored extensively. He went there on each of his three missionary journeys. Each time, he did evangelistic work, founded churches, and began the process of building church leaders.

Paul's epistle to the Galatians reveals that the churches in that region had been subsequently ravaged by legalistic false teachers, known as the *Judaizers,* who corrupted the gospel by teaching that circumcision and other practices borrowed from Old Testament ceremonial law were essential for salvation. Paul's epistle to the Galatians answered those errors but also revealed that the false teaching had become deeply rooted in the Galatian churches.

The fact that Crescens had been sent to such a strategic and difficult field of ministry as Galatia probably indicates that he was a man of great spiritual strength and experience. He was trusted by Paul to give leadership and teaching and to represent Paul in that region where false teachers had already done so much to undermine Paul's influence.

Yet Crescens is virtually unknown. There were undoubtedly many like him who were trusted fellow laborers behind the scenes with Paul, who are never explicitly mentioned in Scripture, but "whose names are in the Book of Life" (Philippians 4:3). No one today remembers their names, but God knows, and they will be fully rewarded for their work. Thus Crescens represents the quiet, unknown hero who comes along in godly maturity and spiritual strength to stand behind someone like Paul and work faithfully without human accolades. I thank the Lord for the multitudes like them who are gifted, called by God, and who in doing their duty are content to be unknown.

Titus

Titus, by contrast, is well-known. His name appears thirteen times in the New Testament. One of Paul's pastoral epistles was written to him and bears his name. Remember (as we saw in an earlier chapter) that Titus was the one who represented Paul in Corinth when the apostle was unable to visit there. Paul wrote of him, "If anyone inquires about Titus, he is my partner and fellow worker concerning you" (2 Corinthians 8:23).

Titus seemed to flourish in new and challenging circumstances. Paul had planted many churches across the Mediterranean region, and when he left to go to the next region, he would turn leadership of the church over to someone like Titus. Titus was an equipper, a builder, and a man who could train other leaders. In fact, when Paul wrote the epistle to Titus, Titus was on the island of Crete, where Paul had planted a church and left it in the capable hands of Titus. Paul wrote to him, "For this reason I left you in Crete, that you should set in order the things that are lacking, and appoint elders in every city as I commanded you" (Titus 1:5).

Titus had been working with Paul for years. He was in close and intimate fellowship with the apostle. Titus 3:12 indicates that Titus left Crete to meet Paul at Nicopolis (probably in northwest Greece). He apparently went from there to Dalmatia at about the same time Paul was being taken to Rome in his final imprisonment. Dalmatia was part of Illyricum, a region on the eastern shore of the Adriatic Sea, north of Macedonia. (Dalmatia is part of modern Croatia and Albania.) Paul had preached in Illyricum, according to Romans 15:19. It was exactly the kind of setting where Titus could go and follow up Paul's missionary work, strengthen the church, and build leaders.

Every person in spiritual service needs not only the quiet, behind-the-scenes helpers like Crescens, but also those (like Titus) who can take a place of prominence. People like Titus are strong builders of other leaders, equippers, reproducers.

Luke

The next name on Paul's list is Luke, Paul's constant and faithful companion. In 2 Timothy 4:11 Paul wrote, "Only Luke is with me." Don't get the idea that Paul was in any way depreciating the character or the importance of Luke. Quite the contrary. Luke was one of the closest and most beloved of Paul's fellow workers. In Colossians 4:14, Paul referred to him as "the beloved physician."

Although Luke's name appears only three times in the New Testament, he is a dominant character in the early church, and especially in Paul's ministry. He wrote the gospel that bears his name, which is the longest of all four Gospels. (Luke's gospel has only twenty-four chapters and Matthew's has twenty-eight, but Luke has more verses and more words than Matthew.) Luke also wrote the entire book of Acts. So fifty-two chapters of the New Testament were penned by this faithful physician, who was also an able historian. He chronicled the life of Christ, and then he chronicled the life of the early church, all under the Holy Spirit's inspiration.

But Luke was obviously humble, and thus he was content to come alongside a great apostle and labor in his shadow. He was a constant companion to Paul, faithfully at his side. He was with Paul on his second missionary journey at Troas and Philippi. He joined Paul at the end of the third missionary journey and went with him to Jerusalem. As we saw throughout the early part of our study, Luke was with Paul in the shipwreck recorded in Acts 27. He remained with Paul through both of his imprisonments. His presence is indicated, starting in Acts 16:10 with the pronoun *we*, indicating that he traveled with Paul from that point on.

Although Luke was an articulate, godly, educated, gifted man, he made himself Paul's servant. His main ministry was to come alongside Paul and serve his personal needs. And if anybody ever needed a personal physician, Paul did. Beaten, stoned, whipped, shipwrecked, imprisoned, and suffering so much, Paul needed a first-rate physician and an intimate friend. That was the role Luke gladly embraced.

Luke apparently wasn't a preacher. There's no record that he ever taught, except through his writing. He doesn't appear to have been a theologian. He was a friend who acted as a personal aide and secretary to Paul and as a historian under the Holy Spirit's inspiration. So the expression "only Luke" does not in any way minimize his value, but simply means that Paul was left with no one other than his personal attendant. For the work that needed to be done, he needed Timothy as well.

Leadership and ministry are greatly enriched by a personal confidant. There probably wasn't anything in Paul's life that Luke didn't know. Luke attended to Paul when the apostle was ill. He stayed with him through every ordeal. He had seen his response in every kind of situation. Theirs was not a nine-to-five association; they had traveled together and worked together for years. Luke was Paul's companion, and he was his closest friend.

These men were all key players in the team Paul had built. They and others like them represented the very heart of Paul's network of beloved people.

THE TRIALS HE SUFFERED

As Paul continued his catalog of people who played a significant role in his life and ministry, he named a few people who, in one way or another, were reminiscent of various trials he had suffered.

Mark

The first of these, Mark, had at one time been a severe personal disappointment and a source of great grief to Paul, but he had since recovered his relationship with the apostle and was now a useful and important fellow laborer. Paul told Timothy, "Get Mark and bring him with you, for he is useful to me for ministry" (2 Timothy 4:11).

Mark is first mentioned in Acts 12:12 (where he's called "John whose surname was Mark"). Luke recorded that many believers had gathered in his mother's home to pray for Peter, who had been imprisoned by Herod. It may be that the church regularly met in Mark's mother's home.

Mark himself was one of the bright, promising young lights in the Jerusalem church. He was chosen to accompany Paul and Barnabas on the first missionary journey. Shortly into the trip, however, according to Acts 13:13, he abandoned the team. Apparently, the hardship was too much for him. He was still immature and didn't have the courage or the character for the rigors of missionary life, so he went home.

Paul had little tolerance for weak, cowardly, or uncommitted men. Therefore, a few years later, when Paul and Barnabas were preparing to depart on their second missionary journey, Paul had no interest in taking Mark with them again. He did not want someone who would be excess baggage, someone who might have to be pushed or carried and might slow them down. This resulted in a sharp dispute between Paul and Barnabas. (According to Colossians 4:10, John Mark was a relative of Barnabas.) Luke recorded what happened:

> Barnabas was determined to take with them John called Mark. But Paul insisted that they should not take with them the one who had departed from them in Pamphylia, and had not gone with them to the work. Then the contention became so sharp that they parted from one another. And so Barnabas took Mark and sailed to Cyprus; but Paul chose Silas and departed, being commended by the brethren to the grace of God. (Acts 15:37–40)

In other words, Paul and Barnabas split over Mark. Barnabas went with Mark, and Paul took Silas. Providentially, this turned out to be a blessing because it resulted in two fruitful missionary teams instead of one, but at the time of the rift with Barnabas, Paul clearly did not anticipate that Mark would ever prove useful.

About twelve years later, when Paul was under house arrest in Rome, he wrote to the church at Colosse. In that epistle, Paul sent this greeting: "Aristarchus my fellow prisoner greets you, with Mark the cousin of Barnabas" (Colossians 4:10). Moreover, he added, "These are my only fellow workers for the kingdom of God who are of the circumcision; they have proved to be a comfort to me" (v. 11). Apparently Mark had proved himself and was back in Paul's good graces—a companion restored.

After that, according to 1 Peter 5:13, Mark also spent time with Peter. Probably it was during that time, at the request of the Roman church, that he wrote his gospel, which strongly reflects the perspective of Peter.

Perhaps when Peter was martyred, Mark returned to labor alongside Paul. He evidently served him well and seems to have been well-known to Timothy. And some twenty years after his original failure, Mark was still faithful. So Paul told Timothy to bring him, "for he is useful to me for ministry."

Useful, because although he had once been the cause of disappointment and conflict for the apostle Paul, he had long since proved himself trustworthy, again and again. Now he was a living reminder of the triumph that comes even through trials. What's more, he was a native Roman. He knew the Roman church and had been part of that flock from the beginning. He could be of great help to Paul in the final days of the apostle's life.

Indeed, one of the great joys in Christian ministry and spiritual leadership is to see someone restored to usefulness after experiencing failure.

Tychicus

The next name in Paul's catalog is Tychicus. "Tychicus I have sent to Ephesus" (2 Timothy 4:12). Tychicus is mentioned four other times in Scripture. We learn from Acts 20:4 that he came from Asia Minor and accompanied Paul to Jerusalem with the offering for the poor saints there. He is also mentioned in Ephesians 6:21, Colossians 4:7, and Titus 3:12. In each case, his special task was to deliver the epistles that Paul wrote. He carried the manuscript of the Ephesian epistle to Ephesus, Colossians to Colossae, and Titus to Crete. In this case, it seems likely that he was also the one delivering 2 Timothy to Ephesus.

Three of these four epistles were written from prison. So Tychicus was apparently, like Luke, one of those who filled a role made necessary by the trials Paul suffered. Because Paul's feet were shackled with chains, Tychicus became Paul's feet for him, delivering vital personal messages to churches Paul himself could not personally visit. But they were more than personal messages; they were the autographs of some of the most important books in the New Testament canon.

Tychicus was given great responsibility, delivering the Word of God to churches; therefore he must have been a loyal and trustworthy man. He himself was evidently not a preacher, but he was nonetheless an important messenger of the truth.

The network of my own ministry is filled with people like Tychicus. I thank God for the people around me who work to disseminate the preaching of God's Word. Most of them do not do what I do, but they make it possible for the message to reach the uttermost parts of the world, by the printed page, through tapes, and on the radio. Every leader needs people like Tychicus. Such people are a wonderful support through every kind of trial.

Carpus

Next on Paul's list is Carpus. Paul told Timothy, "Bring the cloak that I left with Carpus at Troas when you come—and the books, especially the parchments" (2 Timothy 4:13). While Tychicus was the faithful one who traveled for Paul, Carpus was the faithful one who stayed home and played host to the apostle.

Carpus apparently lived in Troas and gave Paul a place to stay during his travels. Paul wanted Timothy to pick up Mark, stop in Troas on the way to Rome, and bring the personal effects Carpus had kept for him.

Troas was north and west of Ephesus in Asia Minor. Paul evidently expected Timothy to travel overland to Greece, then take a ship across the Adriatic to Italy.

Why does Scripture make a point of noting that Paul wanted his cloak? Notice that verse 21 says winter was coming. The cloak was a heavy, square-shaped woolen garment with a hole or a slit in the middle where it went over the head. It could be worn like a poncho or used like a blanket. Paul needed the cloak in that dungeon to keep warm.

That tells us something about Paul's personal economic condition and the poverty of the church in those days. You might think there was no need to trek across Europe with a coat for Paul. But it was obviously more feasible than buying a new one. Besides, Paul wanted the books as well.

Why had he left his cloak at the house of Carpus? Perhaps he didn't want to carry it in the summer. Or perhaps he was arrested suddenly and not given an opportunity even to collect his personal effects. Either way, Carpus becomes another living reminder of the trials Paul suffered, because he was the one lovingly safeguarding Paul's most precious earthly goods while the apostle was imprisoned.

What are the books and parchments Paul refers to? "Parchments" would be important writings preserved on expensive animal-skin scrolls. The "books" were probably papyrus scrolls. Some of them were surely rare personal copies of Old Testament books. Others may have been Paul's own letters, of which he kept copies. Some of them may have even been blanks on which he was about to write other things. The point is clear: Paul wasn't finished reading, writing, and studying, and he wanted his books and papers so that he could redeem the time during his final days on earth.

Paul's network included not only people who formed the core of his team, but also people who ministered to him and encouraged him in his trials. Sadly, there were also a few people in whom he had invested his life who proved to be unfaithful to the Lord and disloyal to Paul personally. He mentioned them as well.

THE TREACHERY HE ENDURED

Rare is the leader who doesn't experience disloyalty and defection. Even Jesus had to endure the treachery of Judas. Usually, betrayal comes from where you least expect it. Paul's experience was no exception to that rule. In fact, the wounds of a good friend's defection were still smarting when he wrote this epistle to Timothy.

Demas

We return now to Demas, whom Paul mentioned in 2 Timothy 4:10: "Demas has forsaken me, having loved this present world, and has departed for Thessalonica."

In fact, Paul mentioned Demas as one of the reasons he needed Timothy to come speedily: "Come to me quickly; for Demas has forsaken me." Why is Demas's defection a reason for asking Timothy to make haste? Could it be that Demas had occupied such a strategic role in Paul's ministry that only Timothy could take his place? The implication is that Timothy needed to come not only for the sake of encouraging Paul, but also for the sake of whatever work had heretofore been Demas's responsibility.

We don't know much about Demas, aside from the fact that he had been with Paul for some time. He is mentioned along with Luke in Colossians 4:14 as one of the esteemed and intimate companions of Paul. While Paul was writing to Colosse during his first imprisonment in Rome, Demas was there. Paul most likely wrote Philemon at about the same time, and Demas is mentioned in verse 24 of that brief epistle too. Along with Mark, Luke, and Aristarchus, Paul named him as a fellow laborer.

So Demas had been associated with Paul at least since that first imprisonment in Rome. He must have been given some kind of important or strategic ministry. He was no doubt someone in whom Paul had invested much. He surely knew much truth. And when he deserted Paul, he left a void that Paul needed Timothy to step into.

The verb translated "forsaken" is the Greek word *egkataleipo*. It is a strong word that speaks of desertion. Its root (*leipo*) means "to leave." It is compounded with two prepositions (*eg* and *kata*, having the sense of "against" and "alone"), making it doubly intense. In this context, it conveys the idea of "leaving me in the lurch." Indeed, Demas had not only abandoned Paul, but he had also left him in a dire situation, at a most inappropriate time.

Perhaps the deprivation had become too much for Demas. It may have been that in the midst of Paul's most extreme difficulty, he could see the handwriting on the wall. Paul was about to lose his life, and apparently Demas wasn't willing to give his life for Christ. He wasn't that committed.

Maybe Demas had first joined Paul because of the noble cause. But he had never really counted the cost. He may well have been like the rocky soil, where the seed has no root in itself, but when tribulation comes, it withers (Mark 4:16–17). Or, more likely, Demas was a classic example of weedy ground, where "the cares of this world, the deceitfulness of riches, and the desires for other things entering in choke the word, and it becomes unfruitful" (v. 19). He probably was never a true Christian at all because Paul said he "loved this present world." And "friendship with the world is enmity with God" (James 4:4). As the apostle John wrote, "If anyone loves the world, the love of the Father is not in him" (1 John 2:15).

Demas had much in common with Judas. He fell in love with the world because he apparently never had any genuine love for Christ. Like Judas, he seemed to follow for a while, but his heart was always in this world.

Why did Demas go to Thessalonica? Most likely, that was his home. Paul linked him with Aristarchus in Philemon, and according to Acts 20:4, Aristarchus was a Thessalonian. Whatever the reason for the place, the reason for his desertion is clear: He loved this world more than he loved Christ.

Virtually every Christian leader will eventually face the desertion of a Demas—someone you pour your life into; you think he is on the team; he is outwardly following Christ; but he brings deep pain and a sense of betrayal when it finally becomes apparent that he loves the present world. This was no reflection on Paul's leadership, any more than Judas reflected negatively on Jesus' leadership.

Alexander the Coppersmith

In 2 Timothy 4:14–15, Paul mentioned another man whose treachery had caused him great grief: "Alexander the coppersmith did me much harm. May the Lord repay him according to his works. You also must beware of him, for he has greatly resisted our words."

Alexander was a common name in the ancient world, so there's no need to assume that this Alexander was the same one mentioned in 1 Timothy 1:20 together with Hymenaeus as a false teacher. Nor do we need to assume that this is the same Alexander mentioned in Acts 19:33, whose testimony sparked a riot. In fact, by referring to him as "Alexander the coppersmith," Paul seemed to set him apart from the other Alexanders. This man was a craftsman who worked with metals. Perhaps he was an idol maker. Remember that a silversmith named Demetrius had once caused a riot in Ephesus, because Paul's preaching was a threat to his idol-making business (Acts 19:24–26).

Whatever Alexander's story, he had caused Paul great harm, and therefore Timothy also needed to be warned to be on guard against him. The nature of the harm he caused is also clear: He opposed Paul's teaching (2 Timothy 4:15). That means he stood against the truth of the gospel.

Notice Paul's response: "May the Lord repay him according to his works" (v. 14). Paul was not asking Timothy to take any action against Alexander, only to beware of him. He did not seek personal vengeance. He did not threaten or revile Alexander in return. Following the example of Christ, he simply "committed Himself to Him who judges righteously" (1 Peter 2:23).

Everyone in leadership and ministry encounters people who set themselves against the truth of God and seek to do us harm. They want to discredit faithful teachers and make them appear as fools, liars, charlatans, or whatever.

Alexander, like Demas, was a living example of the treachery Paul had endured.

The Fainthearted Believers in Rome

There were many more. In verse 16, Paul described how he was abandoned by *everyone* soon after his arrest: "At my first defense no one stood with me, but all forsook me. May it not be charged against them."

We can piece together what had apparently happened from the sparse details Paul gave. He was most likely tracked down and captured somewhere in the Roman Empire, likely far from Rome. Paul may well have been singled out by Nero personally because he had already appeared before the emperor, and he was well-known as a leader of the church. Therefore, when Nero began to persecute Christians, he would have specifically targeted Paul.

Once arrested, Paul would immediately have been transported to Rome for trial. This time Luke probably would not have been permitted to accompany him; the physician would have to arrange his own travel and arrive later.

As soon as Paul reached Rome, he would have been arraigned. The Roman court system demanded that he be given an opportunity to defend himself at that initial hearing. That is most likely what he was describing as his "first defense." It apparently occurred before Luke or Onesiphorus (2 Timothy 1:16), or any of Paul's usual companions were able to reach Rome.

But the church at Rome was filled with believers who knew Paul well. Paul probably anticipated that some of them would testify on his behalf or at least show up at the trial for moral support. But no one did.

"All forsook me." He used the same verb he used to speak of Demas's defection: *egkataleipo*. They left him in the lurch. They abandoned him at a crucial time. They were no doubt embarrassed or afraid to be identified with Paul because of the persecution. Such deliberate neglect of the great apostle who had given so much for them was unthinkable.

Notice Paul's prayer for them: "May it not be charged against them" (v. 16). This makes a stark contrast with his words about Alexander.

That's because Alexander's treachery was driven by evil motives. The people who were no-shows at Paul's defense were most likely driven by their own fears and frailty. They were fainthearted, not false hearted. Paul's wish for them is reminiscent of Stephen, who said of those who were stoning him to death, "Lord, do not charge them with this sin" (Acts 7:60). And it reflects the spirit of Christ, who from the cross prayed, "Father, forgive them, for they do not know what they do" (Luke 23:34).

THE TRIUMPH HE OBTAINED

Abandoned by his friends, hated by his enemies, Paul might have felt like giving up in despair. But instead he wrote:

> The Lord stood with me and strengthened me, so that the message might be preached fully through me, and that all the Gentiles might hear. Also I was delivered out of the mouth of the lion. And the Lord will deliver me from every evil work and preserve me for His heavenly kingdom. To Him be glory forever and ever. Amen! (2 Timothy 4:17–18)

Christ has promised, "I will never leave you nor forsake you" (Hebrews 13:5). Indeed, when everyone else forsook Paul, Christ stood by him.

Paul would have been put on trial in a large basilica teeming with hostile people. Nero himself may have overseen the proceedings, considering the importance of the prisoner. There Paul stood, without an advocate, without any witnesses on his behalf, and with no one to defend him. He was absolutely alone and helpless in front of an imperial court that, from the human point of view, held his life in their hands.

But the Lord stood with him and strengthened him. The Greek verb for "strengthened" speaks of an infusion of power. Paul began to feel Christ's empowerment in his spirit, enabling him to be the human instrument through which the gospel was fully preached, so that all the Gentiles might hear.

That moment was, in effect, the pinnacle of Paul's ministry and the fulfillment of his deepest desire. He was called to be the apostle to the Gentiles. Rome was the cosmopolitan center of the pagan world. Paul had long sought an opportunity to preach the gospel in such a venue before the world's most important political leaders and philosophical trendsetters. This was that opportunity. In the midst of it, Paul was strengthened by the Spirit of Christ to speak boldly and thoroughly.

"I was delivered out of the mouth of the lion," he wrote (v. 17). That's probably figurative language (cf. Psalm 22:21; 35:17) meaning he was spared immediate execution. God delivered him from that perilous tribunal and turned it into an opportunity to preach a strategic gospel message.

But it didn't end his imprisonment or permanently end the danger to Paul's life. He *would* eventually be executed. And he knew that. But notice that even while acknowledging that his death was imminent, the apostle Paul could write, "The Lord will deliver me from every evil work and preserve me for His heavenly kingdom" (v. 18). The deliverance he sought was an eternal reality, not a rescue from temporal or earthly tribulations.

When Paul thought of the certainty of that deliverance, he could not resist a glad expression of worship: "To Him be glory forever and ever. Amen!" (v. 18). This was authentic triumph. And Paul could enjoy it fully despite his circumstances.

Finally, Paul closed both the epistle and the final chapter of his life with some assorted greetings to old friends, news about key ministry partners, and greetings from select people in the church at Rome:

> Greet Prisca and Aquila, and the household of Onesiphorus. Erastus stayed in Corinth, but Trophimus I have left in Miletus sick. Do your utmost to come before winter. Eubulus greets you, as well as Pudens, Linus, Claudia, and all the brethren. The Lord

Jesus Christ be with your spirit. Grace be with you. Amen.
(2 Timothy 4:19–22)

Notice the remaining names of people who also were part of Paul's
extended network:

Priscilla and Aquila

Priscilla and Aquila are familiar to us. They were the couple who worked
with Paul in the tent-making trade during his first visit to Corinth (Acts
18:2–3). They left Corinth with Paul and traveled with him to Ephesus
(vv. 18–19). Having learned so much from Paul, they patiently taught
Apollos (v. 26). Thus Paul's influence extended to Apollos through the
ministry of this couple. They were the instruments God used to help bring
Apollos to maturity, and Apollos became a powerful extension of Paul's
ministry and leadership

When Paul wrote Romans about six years later, Aquila and Priscilla
were living in Rome (Romans 16:3). They apparently left Rome during
the brutal persecution of the Jews carried out by Emperor Claudius. From
there they went back to Ephesus and hosted the Ephesian church in their
house, because when Paul wrote 1 Corinthians (from Ephesus), he sent
greetings to old friends in Corinth on behalf of Aquila and Priscilla and
"the church that is in their house" (1 Corinthians 16:19).

So this was a couple that had traveled extensively with Paul for years.
They were old friends and longtime fellow workers. Paul sent them
greetings.

The Household of Onesiphorus

Onesiphorus may have been in Rome with Paul when Paul sent greetings
back to his household in Ephesus. In 2 Timothy 1:16–17, Paul mentioned
that Onesiphorus had frequently refreshed him without being ashamed
of Paul's imprisonment. Moreover, when Onesiphorus had first come to

Rome, he zealously sought Paul out. He arrived, apparently, soon after that bitter experience at Paul's trial when no one had stood with him. So Paul was obviously very grateful for Onesiphorus's singular kindness to him.

Erastus

Paul then reported that "Erastus stayed in Corinth" (2 Timothy 4:20). This is most likely the same Erastus mentioned in Acts 19:22, who had ministered alongside Timothy in Macedonia. Here was another old friend, a longtime fellow worker, with whom Paul still had a close connection. Now Erastus was apparently helping lead the church in Corinth, and Paul wanted Timothy to stay in contact with him.

Trophimus

Next on Paul's list is another beloved old friend, Trophimus. According to Acts 20:4, Trophimus was from Asia Minor. He also had left his home in order to travel with Paul and work alongside the apostle. He had helped bring the Gentile offering to the poor Christians in Jerusalem. On the way, he traveled through Troas with Paul and was there when Eutychus fell out of the window and was resurrected. When they arrived in Jerusalem, the Jews took notice of Trophimus because he was presumably a Gentile. When they saw Paul in the temple, they wrongly assumed he had Trophimus with him, and that was the incident that led to Paul's first arrest (Acts 21:29).

Now Trophimus was sick, and Paul had left him at Miletus. He must have been rather seriously ill, because Miletus is only about thirty-six miles from his home in Ephesus. We can safely assume that Paul would have healed him if possible. But here is rather dramatic evidence that even before the death of the apostle Paul, the apostolic gifts of healing and miracles ("the signs of an apostle" [2 Corinthians 12:12]) were beginning to cease, or had ceased already. It obviously wasn't the plan of God to heal Trophimus, but Paul had not forgotten his dear friend.

Some Faithful New Friends

In closing, Paul sent greetings from a few believers in Rome who had not been scattered in the persecution: "Eubulus greets you, as well as Pudens, Linus, Claudia, and all the brethren." We know nothing of these people, but they furnish evidence that even in his worst extremity, the apostle Paul's influence was still powerful and active. Even in the worst kind of persecution, people were still coming to Christ, and Paul was still ministering to them.

Finally, here was the sum of Paul's situation: He was in a fetid hole in the ground. Demas was gone. Crescens was ministering elsewhere. Titus was in Dalmatia. Tychicus had been sent to Ephesus. Priscilla, Aquila, Onesiphorus and family, Erastus, and Trophimus were all scattered, carrying on the work Paul had begun. Only Luke was still with the apostle. A few believers in the church at Rome had also lately befriended him. But he longed to see his son in the faith one more time, to finish passing the baton of leadership.

So he said in verse 21, "Do your utmost to come before winter." The appeal is full of pathos and melancholy, even though Paul himself was triumphant. He knew the day of his departure was at hand. Yet he also knew that if Timothy delayed they'd never see each other face-to-face on earth again, and Paul still had much more in his heart to say. Thus the tender plea that sums up and ends this epistle.

Was Paul a failure as a leader? Not in the least. His continuing influence in the lives of so many people gives ample proof of the effectiveness of his leadership to the very end. He had kept the faith. He had fought a good fight. He had finished his course with joy. *That* was his legacy in this life, and through eternity.

ABOUT THE AUTHOR

John MacArthur, the author of numerous best-selling books that have touched millions of lives, is pastor-teacher of Grace Community Church in Sun Valley, California, and president of The Master's College and Seminary. He is also president of Grace to You, the ministry that produces the internationally syndicated radio program *Grace to You* and a host of print, audio, and Internet resources. He authored the notes in the Gold Medallion Award-winning *The MacArthur Study Bible*. John and his wife, Patricia, have four children (all married), who have given them thirteen grandchildren. For more information, contact Grace to You at 1-800-55-GRACE.

Appendix

TWENTY-SIX CHARACTERISTICS OF A TRUE LEADER

1. A LEADER IS TRUSTWORTHY.

2. A LEADER TAKES THE INITIATIVE.

3. A LEADER USES GOOD JUDGMENT.

4. A LEADER SPEAKS WITH AUTHORITY.

5. A LEADER STRENGTHENS OTHERS.

6. A LEADER IS OPTIMISTIC AND ENTHUSIASTIC.

7. A LEADER NEVER COMPROMISES THE ABSOLUTES.

8. A LEADER FOCUSES ON OBJECTIVES, NOT OBSTACLES.

9. A LEADER EMPOWERS BY EXAMPLE.

10. A LEADER CULTIVATES LOYALTY.

11. A LEADER HAS EMPATHY FOR OTHERS.

12. A LEADER KEEPS A CLEAR CONSCIENCE.

13. A LEADER IS DEFINITE AND DECISIVE.

14. A LEADER KNOWS WHEN TO CHANGE HIS MIND.

15. A LEADER DOES NOT ABUSE HIS AUTHORITY.

16. A LEADER DOESN'T ABDICATE HIS ROLE IN THE FACE OF OPPOSITION.

17. A LEADER IS SURE OF HIS CALLING.

18. A LEADER KNOWS HIS OWN LIMITATIONS.

19. A LEADER IS RESILIENT.

20. A LEADER IS PASSIONATE.

21. A LEADER IS COURAGEOUS.

22. A LEADER IS DISCERNING.

23. A LEADER IS DISCIPLINED.

24. A LEADER IS ENERGETIC.

25. A LEADER KNOWS HOW TO DELEGATE.

26. A LEADER IS CHRISTLIKE.

NOTES

Introduction

1. Rich Karlgaard, "Purpose Driven," *Forbes* (February 16, 2004), 39.
2. Ibid.

Chapter 3: Taking Courage

1. Charles Spurgeon, "The Church the World's Hope," *The Metropolitan Tabernacle Pulpit* 51 (London: Passmore & Alabaster, 1905).

Chapter 4: Taking Charge

1. For a fascinating account of the search for this location on Malta, and even the discovery of four anchors, see Robert Cornuke, *The Lost Shipwreck of Paul* (Bend, Ore: Global, 2003).

Chapter 5: A Leader's Devotion to His People

1. I've already written a five-hundred-page commentary on 2 Corinthians, so we don't need to repeat that exercise here. But for those wishing to follow up this book with an even more in-depth look at Paul's approach to leadership in Corinth, see *The MacArthur New Testament Commentary: 2 Corinthians* (Chicago: Moody, 2003).

Chapter 6: Paul Defends His Sincerity

1. Letter CCX1 in Philip Schaff, *The Confessions and Letters of St. Augustine, with a Sketch of his Life and Work.*

Chapter 9: The Leader's Warfare

1. J. Oswald Sanders, *Spiritual Leadership* (Chicago: Moody, 1967), 61.

STUDY GUIDE

CHAPTER 1: EARNING TRUST

"How does a leader build trust? When people are convinced you will do everything in your power for their good and nothing for their harm, they'll trust you."

1. Though a prisoner aboard ship, Paul's natural gift of leadership served to influence those around him. Though enemies, they trusted him. Paul proved himself worthy of their trust. How does 1 Peter 2:11–12 say Christians should act in the midst of a "hostile crew"?

2. Paul is a model of leadership—a natural leader holding great influence over those who surrounded him. But leadership isn't about natural ability. It's about character. What does Romans 5:3–5 tell us about building character?

3. Integrity and reputation go hand in hand. What value does Solomon place on a good reputation, according to Proverbs 22:1 and Ecclesiastes 7:1?

4. In order to earn trust, leaders must show themselves to be people of integrity—respectable, intelligent, and virtuous. When your own life and ministry are marked by these characteristics, what words are assigned to you in Psalm 11:7 and Psalm 32:11?

5. What are the promises you can claim as your own when you live an upright life, according to Psalm 37:18, Psalm 37:37, Psalm 112:2, Psalm 125:4, and Psalm 140:13?

CHAPTER 2: TAKING THE INITIATIVE

"Give me one great, careful, thoughtful, analytical, wise leader over the majority anytime."

1. An effective leader needs more than charisma and clever words. Solomon knew this more than any other leader. What was his heart's desire, according to 1 Kings 3:5–9? In what ways do his desires mirror your own as you lead?

2. What was the psalmist's prayer in Psalm 119:66? For what specific situations do you need to pray these same words?

3. John MacArthur writes, "[Nehemiah] was sincere and believable. His enthusiasm was infectious. His optimism was contagious. They caught the vision." How can you emulate Nehemiah and inspire enthusiasm in the hearts of those you lead?

4. Good leaders have foresight—they chart a path and plan ahead. What do Proverbs 15:22, 19:21, 20:18, and 21:5 have to say about the plans that come naturally to you?

5. As we seek wisdom in taking the initiative to lead, what truth does Proverbs 16:9 remind us to consider?

CHAPTER 3: TAKING COURAGE

"As a true leader, Paul saw beyond the temporary circumstances and fixed his hope on the promise of triumph. And he drew courage and confidence from that. Such optimism was contagious."

1. Leaders inspire confidence, but confidence can be misplaced. What kind of person is unworthy of confidence, according to Proverbs 25:19? What can we safely place our confidence in, according to 1 John 2:28 and 5:14?

2. As a leader, Paul exuded authority. His commanding air spoke of boldness and conviction. What was his prayer, according to Philippians 1:20? According to 2 Corinthians 3:12, what is our source of boldness?

3. When Paul confronted the Corinthian church, his purpose was not to chide, but to cheer up. "A real leader's aim is to make everyone around him better. He makes them stronger, more effective, and more motivated." How does Paul describe the two-fold ministry of Timothy in 1 Thessalonians 3:2? What is the balance between these two aspects in your own leading?

4. When Jesus walked the earth, He amazed the masses because He spoke with such authority. Where does all true authority come from, according to Romans 13:1?

5. John MacArthur writes, "The amazing authority with which Paul spoke was an unshakable authority derived from his absolute certainty that God's Word was true and His promises were trustworthy." What happens when you, in your position of authority, lead with courage and integrity, according to Proverbs 29:2?

CHAPTER 4: TAKING CHARGE

"The real leader is the one who can handle the stress. He is the one who can solve the problems, bear the burdens, find the solutions, and win the victories when everyone else is merely flustered, confounded, and perplexed."

1. Paul's composure in the face of an imminent shipwreck was a mark of his ability to lead. In the midst of a crisis, he was the only one with a clue what to do. What does Paul invite us to do, according to Philippians 3:17, effectively making himself a mentor for generations of leaders to come?

2. Paul took charge and became an example to all those who are called to be leaders. What does he tell us about the pattern he set in 1 Timothy 1:16, 2 Timothy 1:13, and Titus 2:7?

3. Leaders set an example for those who follow after them. In what areas does Paul encourage you to shine as an example for others, according to 1 Timothy 4:12?

4. Even before Paul and Timothy rose up as leaders, the Lord set an example for all those who would follow after. What do John 13:15 and 1 Peter 2:21 urge you to do?

5. A leader focuses on objectives, not obstacles. What does Philippians 3:12–14 have to teach us about keeping our eyes clearly fixed forward? How can this perspective help you to overcome the obstacles in your own path?

CHAPTER 5: A LEADER'S DEVOTION TO HIS PEOPLE

"The wise leader cultivates loyalty by being loyal—loyal to the Lord, loyal to the truth, and loyal to the people he leads."

1. "What do we mean by loyalty? Authentic loyalty is not blind devotion to a mere man. It is, first of all, an allegiance to truth and duty." God Himself sets the standard for true loyalty and faithfulness. What do 2 Timothy 2:13, 1 Thessalonians 5:24, and 2 Thessalonians 3:3 tell us about our Heavenly Father?

2. "Leadership is all about motivating people to follow. Therefore everything in leadership hinges on the leader's relationship to his people." Scripture often compares the relationship of a leader and his people to that of a shepherd with his flock. What are the sure signs that your own shepherding is of the "good" variety, according to Isaiah 40:11, Ezekiel 34:12, and John 10:11?

3. "Leadership hinges on trust, and trust is cultivated by loyalty." How can you inspire loyalty in those who follow you, according to John 10:14 and 1 Peter 5:2–4?

4. When you consider the call to leaders given in Acts 20:28, how does that change your perspective and encourage you to lead differently?

5. Leadership is ultimately about people, not just sterile objectives and strategies that can be written on paper. That means caring—loving. Who are the people that come to mind when love and leadership are described so practically in Romans 12:10–15?

CHAPTER 6: PAUL DEFENDS
HIS SINCERITY

"Good leaders must be able to make decisions in a way that is clear-headed, proactive, and conclusive. They must also be able to communicate objectives in a way that is articulate, emphatic, and distinct. After all, a leader is someone who leads."

1. Paul's leadership was marked by clear convictions. There was no vacillating in his life. How does Paul describe his surety in 2 Timothy 1:12?

2. Those who vacillate cannot be relied upon by others. How is such a life described in James 1:6–8? In what areas of your life do you crave greater consistency?

3. Far better is the steadfast life—consistent, straightforward, sincere. How do 1 Corinthians 15:58, Colossians 1:21–23, and Hebrews 3:14 urge you on to a steadfast life?

4. Paul backed up his words with a life that was dependable and wholly in harmony with what he taught. What is the clear message of Romans 2:13 and James 1:22 in this regard?

5. Paul's words were always plain, honest, forthright, unflinching, and nonevasive—just like the apostle himself. That inspired confidence in those he taught. We too must walk worthy of the message we bring. What do Ephesians 4:1–2, Colossians 1:10, and 1 Thessalonians 2:12 have to say on this score?

CHAPTER 7: "WHO IS SUFFICIENT FOR THESE THINGS?"

"Such confidence is a great and necessary strength in leadership—to be so secure in your giftedness, so emphatic about your calling that no trial, however severe, could ever make you question your life's work. Effective leadership depends on that kind of resoluteness, courage, boldness, and determination."

1. Paul was being attacked on several fronts: his character, his influence, his calling, and his humility. But Paul was sure of his calling. He knew He'd been chosen by God despite his limitations. What do 1 Corinthians 1:27–28 and James 2:5 teach us about those God chooses?

2. "Paul was certain of his calling. That is why he refused to abdicate his leadership to the false teachers. His calling was a stewardship received from God." What can you be assured of in your own calling to lead, according to Romans 11:29 and 2 Timothy 1:9?

3. Although Paul was supremely confident of his calling and quite sure of his own giftedness, he also remembered where those gifts had come from, and he knew they were not from within himself. The source of his adequacy was God. What is Paul's prayer for the called in 2 Thessalonians 1:11?

4. "Paul was a flesh-and-blood, living, walking testimony. His credentials as a leader were written in the lives of the Corinthians themselves. The influence of his ministry on their lives was ample proof of the legitimacy and the effectiveness of his leadership." Chosen, called, and appointed to the task of leading. What does Paul share about his appointed place in the Corinthians' lives in 2 Corinthians 10:13? What is your place in the lives of those you lead?

5. In Revelation 17:14, what three terms are used to describe those who are with Jesus? Does knowing this affect your own goals and aspirations for living and leading?

CHAPTER 8: A LEADER MADE OF CLAY

"No true leader can boast of having attained his position merely because of superior talents, physical attributes, communication skills, or whatever. If God did not use homely, ordinary clay pots, there wouldn't be any spiritual leaders at all, because there aren't any people who aren't beset with blemishes and human weaknesses."

1. Paul's detractors worked to undermine his reputation, forcing him to refute false accusations and "boast" of his position as an apostle. But Paul's words were not true boasting. It was, quite frankly, a matter of constant amazement to Paul himself that he was ever called to leadership to begin with. How does 1 Timothy 1:12–13 explain this astonishment?

2. Paul's attitude echoed that of the psalmist: "My soul shall make its boast in the Lord" (Ps. 34:2 NKJV). What were the things Paul deemed worthy of boasting, according to 2 Corinthians 12:9 and Galatians 6:14?

3. We are vessels—just clay pots. How does the Lord refer to Paul in Acts 9:15?

4. Paul was well aware of all the imperfections in his life, but his weaknesses were not an obstacle to leading. He said they equipped him. By using common, ordinary clay pots, God puts His glory on display in bold relief. How can this be true in your own leading, according to 2 Corinthians 12:9–10?

5. Our weakness doesn't prove fatal to the cause of truth. In fact, it is advantageous, because it gets us out of the way and lets the power of God do the work. How does 2 Corinthians 4:7 shift your mindset concerning any obstacles and weaknesses you are currently struggling with?

CHAPTER 9: THE LEADER'S WARFARE

"Spiritual warfare is all about demolishing evil lies with the truth. Use the authority of God's Word and the power of the gospel to give people the truth. That is what will pull down the fortresses of falsehood. That is the real nature of spiritual warfare."

1. Leaders must harness their passions rather than be harnessed by them. Zeal must be focused, carefully governed, and used for godly purpose. What does Paul say must be done with these passions in Galatians 5:24?

2. How is this idea further explained in Colossians 3:5?

3. Solomon knew the wisdom of self-control. How do Proverbs 16:32 and Proverbs 25:28 describe people who have learned not to be ruled by their appetites?

4. Being misrepresented, slandered, reviled, persecuted, and wrongfully accused is an inevitable part of being a Christian. We must expect to suffer unjustly, for it is a part of the spiritual battle we are in. Paul uses the language of warfare in his letters. What terms do we find in 1 Timothy 1:18, 1 Thessalonians 5:8, and 2 Timothy 2:3? Does knowing you're in a battle change your attitude toward living and leading?

5. Paul knew the real battle was not merely against the human false teachers who had confused the Corinthians. It was nothing less than full-scale war against the kingdom of darkness. How is our fight described in 2 Corinthians 10:3?

CHAPTER 10: HOW NOT TO BE DISQUALIFIED

"Self-control is absolutely vital to lasting success in any endeavor of life. Many people do attain a degree of prominence on the strength of sheer natural talent alone. But the real, influential leaders are the ones who devote themselves to personal discipline and make the most of their gifts."

1. Perhaps the greatest pitfall for those in positions of leadership comes in the form of personal discipline. To explain this idea, Paul compares believers to athletes and our Christian life to a race. What imagery does Paul use in Philippians 2:16 and 2 Timothy 2:5?

2. The price of victory is discipline. That means self-control, sacrifice, and hard work. It's a lifelong commitment for all who would lead. What does Paul say about his own "race" in Philippians 3:12?

3. Discipline has to become a passion. It isn't merely a question of doing whatever is mandatory and avoiding whatever is prohibited. It involves voluntary self-denial. What have you willingly laid aside in order to better lead? How does Paul describe those who compete for an imperishable crown in 1 Corinthians 9:25?

4. What is another analogy Paul uses in describing our struggle against our own sinfulness, as found in Romans 6:19?

5. If we want to finish the race set before us, careful, relentless self-discipline is required. What does Paul urge us to do in 1 Timothy 4:7? And what should we be willing to sacrifice to reach the finish line, according to Acts 20:24?

CHAPTER 11: WHO IS FIT TO LEAD?

"A person whose Christian testimony is free from the taint of scandal—someone who is upright, sound in character, and without any serious moral blemish. Simply put, it means leaders must have a reputation for unimpeachable integrity."

1. When it comes to fitness for leadership, purity, not personality, is the key issue. Those who wish to lead must be found blameless. What do Philippians 2:15 and 1 Thessalonians 5:23 have to say on this subject?

2. What are we urged to do in 2 Peter 3:14?

3. In the New Testament church, team leadership was the norm. Invariably, there would be those, like Paul, who would have more influence in their role. This is just the natural expression of his God-given gifts and abilities. What do we learn about the diversity of spiritual gifts in Romans 12:6, 1 Corinthians 12:4, and 1 Corinthians 14:12? How is this diversity expressed in your own leadership team?

4. All people are differently equipped, but from this diversity God crafts the unity that is the Church. How does Paul describe our place in the Body of Christ in Romans 12:4 and 1 Corinthians 12:18?

5. It is God's plan that those who lead and those who follow be found working together. How does Ephesians 4:16 describe this unique unity? How can you help foster this kind of unity with those who lead with you and those who follow your lead?

CHAPTER 12: THE MEASURE
OF A LEADER'S SUCCESS

"Paul measured his own success as a leader, as an apostle, and as a Christian by a single criterion: He had 'kept the faith'—meaning both that he had remained faithful to Christ and that he had kept the message of Christ's gospel intact, just as he had received it."

1. Paul's legacy in leadership is one of faithfulness. What did he thank God for in 1 Timothy 1:12?

2. The measure of success we seek is very different from that of the world. Like Paul, we must seek to be counted faithful by the Lord. Where does this legacy of faithfulness often find its start, according to Luke 16:10?

3. How is your legacy of faithfulness extended, according to 2 Timothy 2:2?

4. Paul was able to lead with confidence because he kept his eyes clearly fixed on the goal. The end was always in his sights. What do Romans 6:22 and 1 Peter 1:9 say is waiting for us at the end? And what do Matthew 24:13, Hebrews 3:6, and Hebrews 6:11 encourage us to do as we move toward that end?

5. Was Paul a failure as a leader? Not in the least. He had kept the faith. He had fought a good fight. He had finished his course with joy. That was his legacy in this life, and through eternity. What words can we be sure he'll be hearing from the mouth of his Lord, as found in Matthew 25:21?